THE SPIRITUALITY OF JUDAISM

Religious Experience Series

Edward J. Malatesta, S.J., General Editor

Volume	1	Jesus in Christian Devotion and Contemplation
Volume	2	A Christian Anthropology
Volume	3	The Revelations of Divine Love of Julian of Norwich
Volume	4	How to Pray Today
Volume	5	Imitating Christ
Volume	6	Paths to Contemplation
Volume	7	Celibacy for Our Times
Volume	8	The Mysticism of *The Cloud of Unknowing*
Volume	9	The Religious Experience of Jesus and His Disciples
Volume	10	The Depth of God
Volume	11	The Spirituality of Judaism
Volume	12	Jesus Christ in Our World

Religious Experience Series No. 11

THE SPIRITUALITY OF JUDAISM

ROGER Le DÉAUT C.S.Sp.,
ANNIE JAUBERT KURT HRUBY

Translated by
PAUL BARRETT O.F.M. Cap.

ANTHONY CLARKE
WHEATHAMPSTEAD HERTFORDSHIRE

Le Judaïsme, of which this is a translation, appeared originally in the *Dictionnaire de Spiritualité* and published subsequently in book form by Beauchesne, Paris, 1975

This edition first published 1977
ANTHONY CLARKE BOOKS
Wheathampstead, Hertfordshire, England
also published in U.S.A. by Abbey Press, St. Meinrad, Indiana

Unless otherwise noted, Scripture quotations are from the Revised Standard Version Bible Catholic Edition © 1966 and used by permission

ISBN 0 85650 046 1

MADE AND PRINTED IN GREAT BRITAIN BY CHAPEL RIVER PRESS ANDOVER HAMPSHIRE

Preface

Pope Pius XII once said that we Christians are spiritual Semites, while more recently John XXIII, Paul VI and the Second Vatican Council stressed the need for more fraternal understanding and better ecumenical relationships between Christians and their Jewish brethren.

This is the spirit in which the present volume is offered. It tries to clarify numerous passages from Sacred Scripture and to suggest that they be reread in such a way as to take account of the history of the race from which Christ sprang, as well as of the religious climate in which He was nurtured. Thus, for example, St. Luke tells us that Christ used to attend the synagogue and that He followed the tradition of commenting on the Law and the Prophets (Lk 4:16).

In addition, these pages are intended to further the dialogue between Christians and Jews which happily has already made great progress.

We have tried to show the development of Jewish religious and spiritual life during the long history of the race. Because of its great diversity, Jewish spirituality has often been misunderstood, and its depth and richness will perhaps surprise those who encounter it for the first time. But we hope that their surprise will give way to the joy of knowledge which leads to an opening up of the mind and heart.

Roger Le Déaut, C.S.Sp.,
Professor at the Biblical Institute, Rome

Annie Jaubert,
Director of Research at the National Center for Scientific Research, Paris

Kurt Hruby,
Professor at the Catholic Institute, Paris

Translator's Note

Footnotes and bibliographies (by chapters) will be found at the end of the book. I have ventured to insert short explanatory notes into the text whenever I thought they would be of interest to the reader. I have marked these insertions off by enclosing them in square brackets, like this [. . . .]; and, naturally, I take sole responsibility for any errors they may contain.

List of Abbreviations

DS	*Dictionnaire de Spiritualité*
JA	Josephus, Flavius: *Jewish Antiquities*
JW	Josephus, Flavius: *The Jewish War*
M.	*Mishnah*
R.	Rabbi
T.	*Targum*

Table of Contents

		Preface	v
		Translator's Note	vi
		List of Abbreviations	vi
		INTRODUCTION	1
CHAPTER	I.	HISTORY AND RELIGIOUS DEVELOPMENT	3
		by Roger Le Déaut, C.S.Sp.	
		A. Exile and Restoration	3
		B. The Hellenistic Era	6
		C. The Roman Occupation	9
		D. Rabbinical Judaism	14
CHAPTER	II.	RELATIONSHIPS WITH GOD	15
		by Annie Jaubert	
		A. The Covenant	15
		B. The Law	17
		C. Sin and Grace	19
		D. Experiencing and Knowing God	22
CHAPTER	III.	WORSHIP AND RELIGIOUS PRACTICES	25
		by Roger Le Déaut, C.S.Sp.	
		A. The Role of the Temple	25
		B. The Feasts	31
		C. The Liturgy of the Synagogue, and Prayer	36
		D. Fasting and Asceticism	39

CHAPTER IV. RELATIONSHIPS WITH MEN 41
by Annie Jaubert
A. The Brotherhood of the Israelites 41
B. Attitude Towards the Gentiles 45

CHAPTER V. TRADITIONAL TEACHING 49
by Kurt Hruby*
A. Starting Point 50
B. Contents of Tradition 52
C. The Need for Interpreting Scripture 53
D. The Relationships Between the Two Branches of Revelation 55
E. Method of Handing Down Tradition 56

CHAPTER VI. THE TORAH 59
A. The Gift of the Torah 59
B. The Study of the Torah 62
C. Life According to the Torah 63
D. Praise of the Torah and Study 66

CHAPTER VII. PRAYER AND PIETY 69
A. Prayer, Piety and the Torah 69
B. The Structure of Prayer 69
C. The Synagogue Takes Over 70
D. Evolution of the Liturgy 72
E. The Language of Prayer 74
F. The Value of Prayer 74

CHAPTER VIII. TRENDS IN SPIRITUALITY 77
A. The Esoteric Trend 77
B. The Blending of the Esoteric Current with Tradition 80
C. The Influence of Religious Philosophy 81
D. German Hassidism 82

CHAPTER IX. THE KABBALAH 85
A. Development 85

---

* Kurt Hruby is the author of Chapters V through X.

B. The "Discovery" of the *Zohar* 87
C. The Kabbalah after the Discovery of the *Zohar* 88
D. The "Cenacle of Safed" and "Holy Ari" 89
E. The Kabbalistic System of the *Zohar*, and Luria's Contributions 90
F. Ari's *Musar* and the Victory of His Kabbalah 94

CHAPTER X. SPIRITUAL DEVELOPMENT AFTER ARI 99
A. General Situation: Shabbataï Ṣevi 99
B. Polish Hassidism 100
C. Development of Hassidism 104
D. The Life-Style of the *Ḥassidim* 106
E. Modern Times 107

APPENDIX SOURCES 113
by Roger Le Déaut, C.S.Sp.
A. The Later Protocanonical and Deuterocanonical Books 113
B. The Apocrypha (Pseudepigrapha) 115
C. The Writings of Hellenistic Judaism 116
D. The Writings Found in the Desert of Judah 117
E. The New Testament 117
F. Ancient Rabbinical Literature 118
G. The Jewish Liturgy 119

Notes 121

Bibliography 130

Introduction

Judaism, as distinct from the ancient Jewish religion, began to take shape after the Exile [which ended in 539 B.C.] in the Persian era, mainly as a result of the activity of Nehemiah and Ezra (Esdras), about 445 to 400 B.C. The term "Judaism" itself (2 Mc 2:21; 8:1; 14:38) seems to have been coined by the Greek-speaking Jews to distinguish themselves from other groups in the world of Hellenism.

In fact, the Exile and restoration mark a turning point in the history of Israel. A process of evolution, in which the ups and downs of history played a large part, gave Israel new traits which were accentuated during the Maccabean era. Existing institutions underwent changes and new institutions were begun, while various trends and movements became more clearly defined. All of this went to make up the multifaceted Judaism from which Christianity sprang.

But for Israel the course of history continued to flow. Due to the failure of the revolts of 66-73 A.D. and 132-135 A.D., there was a return to, and a hardening in, the positions of Pharisaism, which from then on became, for all practical purposes, the only form of Judaism to be reckoned with and the one from which rabbinical Judaism arose.

Therefore, if we are not to be guilty of anachronisms, unwarranted transpositions and undue generalizations in trying to describe the spirituality of Judaism, we must distinguish clearly between the different periods while being careful to keep in mind their essential continuity.

First, we shall sketch in broad outline the historical development of ancient Judaism; then we shall discuss some basic elements of the Jewish religion; after that, we shall follow the evolution of Jewish spirituality up to the present day; and finally, in an appendix, we shall survey the principal sources.

Chapter I

History and Religious Development

by Roger Le Déaut, C.S.Sp.

Biblical revelation has always been intimately connected with history, and so the religion of Israel is also the reflection of her history. The history of Judaism begins with the Exile, which marked the end of the Jewish *nation.* The new Israel, after the restoration, was no longer the same as before: it was no longer a very small ethnic group living within the boundaries of Palestine but a *religious* community which, spreading out from such important centers as Alexandria and Babylonia, was to make its presence felt throughout the ancient world.

A. Exile and Restoration (587 to 333 B.C.)

It is impossible to understand Judaism without taking into account the impact of the Exile, which provoked a crisis of faith among Jews, jolting them into becoming more spiritual-minded. Deportation caused them to reflect on God's dealings with His people, the very meaning of Israel, their election as the Chosen People, their history and mission, the implications of the covenant and God's promises, the meaning of the gift of the earth, and the role of the Temple and its worship. Jeremiah and Ezekiel were to be the principal authors of the new theology that would lay the foundation for the reform of Nehemiah-Ezra. From this point on, the essential things were not to be the Temple and the dynasty of David, upon which the preceding generations had pinned their hopes in every grave crisis.

According to the prophets, the ultimate cause of Israel's misfortunes was infidelity to Yahweh. The Jews, therefore, returned to a scrupulous observance of His precepts. From the time of the Exile, special stress was laid on those practices which marked Israel off from the pagans, especially the custom of circumcision and the observance of the Sabbath, which from then on were to be the only safeguards of Jewish identity (Jer 17:19-27; Is 56:1-8; 58:13; Ez 20:12). In strange, "unclean" lands, the Jews fostered a special solicitude for ritual purity and for the distinction between the sacred and the profane (Ez 22:26; 44). In Ezekiel, the promise of a new heart is accompanied by the promise of the spirit of God that will "cause you to walk in my statutes and be careful to observe my ordinances" (Ez 36:25-27).

The Jews' encounter with different cultures and religions made them realize more clearly their mission as sons of Abraham and caused them to appreciate more vividly the unique character of the revelation contained in their sacred books and traditions. Some borrowings in the area of knowledge about the angels and the afterlife, a certain degree of distinction between matter and spirit, as well as the concept of reward and punishment after death, and even the very idea of the resurrection of the body, may have passed into biblical revelation as a result of contact with the Iranian religion. This association with the Gentile nations gave rise to a universalist, even a missionary, openness (Is 56:1-8; 66:18-21), which, nevertheless, was largely negated by the particularist and separatist tendencies that were so natural in an exiled people striving to retain their identity.

[Surprisingly enough, the concepts of the immortality of the soul and of reward and punishment after death are not found in most of the Old Testament. Generally speaking, the virtuous man is pictured as being rewarded with long life on earth, health, wealth and many children; and the sinner is punished by being deprived of these benefits. The ancient Hebrews, certainly until after the Exile, viewed death as the end of man's real existence, and his only hope of immortality was to live on in his children. They did have the concept of Sheol, a place in which men, both good and bad, existed after death as shadows, like mournful ghosts drifting through a cold grey mist, in a semiconscious state at most, not completely nonexistent, yet by no means fully alive. Everyone ended up in Sheol, where both the good and evil things of life ceased to delight or torture. The ancient Israelites had no concept of a spiritual principle, that is, a soul, that could live on after the death of the body. The nearest they came to it was the hope that the *body* would rise again; and even then, not only the virtuous but also the wicked would rise to a new life in a new world. The Old Testament comes closest to the Christian idea of the immortality of the soul in the Book of Wisdom, the author of which may have adopted Greek thought on the subject. But Wisdom was the last book of the Old Testament to be written and dates from about 100-50 B.C.]

The face of Judaism was also marked by the disillusionments of the restoration. [The first Temple, that is, the one built by Solomon between 968 and 961 B.C., had stood until 587 B.C., when Nebuchadnezzar, King of Babylon, had destroyed it (2 Kgs 25:9).] The second Temple, which had been started so enthusiastically in 537 B.C., was not finished until 515 B.C., and, despite the hopes of Zerubbabel and the high priest, Joshua, and the exhortations of Haggai and Zechariah, it was clear that only a pale shadow of past glories would be recaptured. Malachi even paints a dark picture of the decadence of the priesthood and worship. Israel had to fight for survival, not only against the hostile Samaritans, but also against those Jews who had not experienced the Exile and whose religion had declined greatly (Hg 2:10-14; Ezr 6:21). Israel had to draw clear lines of demarcation between herself and the other nations so as not to lose her identity by merging with them. The ramparts of Jerusalem, rebuilt since the first mission of Nehemiah (445-433 B.C.), were, so to say, symbolic of the measures of protection that had to be taken from then on, such as forbidding mixed marriages (Ezr 9-10), and condemning negligence in worship and the keeping of the Sabbath (Neh 13).

But while Nehemiah, with the support of the Persian king, succeeded in restoring political status to the Jews, religious reform was the work of Ezra, the priest-scribe, who was given the mission of instructing the people to observe the law of God under pain of the same punishments dealt out to those who condemned "the law of the king" (Ezr 7:25-26). Ezra can be considered the founder of Judaism, and traditionally he was compared to Moses.[1] He impressed on the faith of Israel certain traits that were to be preserved down through the centuries, especially that of making the Law the rallying point of the community. The Jew would no longer be marked out by belonging to one nation or by his participation in the Temple worship, which was impossible for the members of the Diaspora, but by his acceptance and observance of the Law (Neh 9-10).

B. The Hellenistic Era
(333 to 63 B.C.)

Alexander the Great's conquest put an end to the Persian empire, in which Judea had been a semi-independent theocratic state under the authority of the high priests and the Persian governor. However, we have almost no information about the life of the Jewish community in this period until the beginning of the narrative contained in the Books of the Maccabees in 175 B.C. The main event of this time was the massive invasion of Greek culture and customs, that is, of Hellenism, which Alexander wished to impose on the countries he conquered so as to bind his empire together. Greek then replaced Aramaic as the *lingua franca* of the Near East.

Alexander the Great died in 323 B.C. and from his empire came three kingdoms, two of which, that of the Seleucids of Syria and the Ptolemies of Egypt, were to have a decisive influence on the history and religion of the Jews during the three centuries preceding the Christian era. As successive rulers of Palestine, first the Ptolemies and then the Seleucids practiced a policy of toleration. Judaism and Hellenism, far from confronting each other, developed and mingled harmoniously together. This was a dangerous time for the Jewish faith because the appeal of the new culture, then so fashionable, could have led to the rejection of the ancient customs. The aristocracy and the priesthood were especially receptive to the new influences. This type of voluntary Hellenization, which was to reappear under the Hasmoneans, must be distinguished from the Hellenization which Antiochus IV Epiphanes (from 167 B.C. onwards) and the high priests in the pay of the Seleucids tried to impose and which sparked the revolt of the Maccabees, a revolt which was to allow Judaism to free itself from the Greek danger and, when it had defined its own true nature, to assimilate without risk all the benefits of Hellenism. Later, under Herod, orthodox Jews would frequent the theatres and gymnasiums of Alexandria and Jerusalem, and many of the Greek ideas were to infiltrate the Jewish system of thought, but an unquestioned monotheism and the supremacy of the Torah safeguarded the essence of the Jewish religion.

The dispersion of the Jews among other nations was a prime factor in the history of Judaism. Hellenization among these Jews of the Diaspora was to be expected. It had begun quite early, as can be seen from Egyptian documents. Ptolemy I settled Jews in Egypt, where they made steady progress. But Jewish colonies were to be found almost everywhere. Judaism owes to the Diaspora the organization of communities which served as a basis for active propaganda and proselytism among the pagans;[2] and it owes to the same source a literature which showed that it could be adapted to other cultures. Finally, Judaism is indebted to the Diaspora for a Greek Bible, which, along with the works of Philo of Alexandria, was perhaps the most important attempt at a dialogue, of which, however, Christianity was to be the chief beneficiary.

Some marked aspects of the Judaism of this era deserve to be noted particularly. The failure of various institutions or the growth of new attitudes towards them led to the concentration of piety and religious dynamism on the knowledge and practice of the Torah (see below, Chapter 6). The continuation of the prophets' work was, in a sense, ensured by the lay scribe, the doctor or teacher of the Law, who became the spiritual director of the people (Sir 39:1-11), while the priest's main function was to perform the rites of worship. The synagogue, which originated with the Exile, was a center of worship and learning, and soon it assumed the important role it was to play in Judaism by helping to ensure a certain unity in those areas.[3] Gradually, Israel was going through the stages that would make Judaism the religion of the Book and the Law.

The crisis in the ancient Jewish institutions was centered principally on the priesthood. The legitimate high priests, descended from Aaron and Zadok, fell into disrepute under Antiochus IV Epiphanes and his successors, and Ben Sira's eulogy of Simon II (Sir 50:1-21) may be considered the swan song of an era that would never return. This period, during which the high priesthood went to the highest bidder, was simply the prelude to one in which the priesthood would be completely subject to those in political power, to Herod and the Roman procurators, who selected and deposed the high priest at will.

During this time, the supreme religious authority was in the hands of the Sanhedrin,[4] in which the influence of the Pharisees gradually increased. The Pharisees developed the concept of an oral law stretching back to Moses in person, and this became the main point of friction between them and the Sadducees.[5] When problems arose to which traditional theology could no longer give a satisfactory answer or, especially, a sufficiently explicit answer, the Scriptures were consulted. (The *midrash,* or commentary, was already present in the later parts of the Old Testament.) A vast amount of work was done in "rereading," codifying and fixing traditions and in constant application of the prophetical books to current affairs, a practice which the apocalyptic trend would prolong. This ease in reading the meaning of history in the prophets is abundantly illustrated in the *pesharim* ("commentaries") of Qumran and in the New Testament itself, as well as in the increasingly emotive forms in which messianism and eschatological speculations were presented. The persecutions of the era of the Maccabees turned Jewish thought towards the next world and helped to harden belief in the resurrection of the body (2 Mc 7). At the same time, a theology of martyrdom began to be evolved which would inspire the *Ascension of Isaiah* and would pass over into Christianity. [The *Ascension of Isaiah* was an apocryphal life of Isaiah written in the first century A.D. In it,

Isaiah is depicted as having had visions of Christ and the Church.] The spiritual ferment taking place in Judaism showed itself also in a fragmentation that became fully evident during the following era, as well as in the appearance of much apocryphal writing in which the supporters of the various trends expressed their religious views.

C. The Roman Occupation

The Hasmonean dynasty, descendants of the Maccabees, ruled Palestine until Pompey arrived in 63 B.C. to put an end to the power struggle between Aristobulus II and Hyrcanus II, the two sons of Salome Alexandra (reigned 76-69 B.C.). Hyrcanus II won the support of Antipater, governor of Idumea, whose son, Herod the Great (reigned 37-4 B.C.), was to take over, with Rome's approval, the power which the last Hasmoneans had so misused. The troubles that followed Herod's death compelled the Romans to intervene again, and his kingdom was divided between his three sons. Archelaus was made ruler of Judea, but he was deposed by Caesar Augustus in 6 A.D., and Judea was thenceforth governed by Roman procurators, of whom the best known was Pontius Pilate, the fifth procurator, who ruled from 27 until 37 A.D. The almost constant political unrest degenerated into outright rebellion and led to the first Jewish War (66-73 A.D.), with the occupation of Jerusalem and the destruction of the Temple in 70 A.D. War broke out again under the Emperor Hadrian for reasons that are still uncertain, and the revolt, which was led by Ben Kosba (Bar Kochba) with the support of Rabbi 'Aqiba, lasted from 132 to 135 A.D. and ended in the destruction of the Jewish nation. Jerusalem was renamed Aelia Capitolina and forbidden to the Jews, for whom a new era then began.

We must stress here the religious motives which, along with other factors, inspired those who took an active part in the rebellion, one such motive being the desire to rid the Holy Land of pagan rule. The messianic aura surrounding Bar Kochba, as well as the participation and savage resistance by "pacifists" such as the Essenes, shows that these outbreaks were primarily religious wars inspired by faith in God's promises to His chosen people. Every time Jerusalem was even temporarily freed, religious practices were resumed. Thus, coins were struck but without any human likeness on them. Those places where resistance was strongest became religious centers in which the laws and ritual practices were scrupulously observed. In the lament of the conquered Jews after the first revolt we can hear the cry of a faith that is questioning itself: "Sion has been taken from us. The Almighty and His law are our only inheritance."[6]

Of the various aspects of the Judaism of the first century A.D., we shall stress only the diversity which had already begun to appear in it during the preceding era. This was a Judaism of transition containing a large number of trends which rabbinical Judaism was to assimilate or reject. These movements or trends were much more complex than the well-known division by Flavius Josephus [into Pharisees, Sadducees and Essenes] would lead us to suppose.[7] We shall mention only the most important of these movements.

1. The Pharisees

No doubt the Pharisees derive from that group of the *Ḥassidim* ("pious ones") who gathered around the Maccabees (1 Mc 2:42). They were defenders of the Law and of the oral tradition that formed a barrier around it.[8] They were the real educators of the people. According to Josephus, who was perhaps inclined to exaggerate their influence, the public held them in great esteem.[9] They can be described in brief as the virtuosos of Jewish piety. Although both the New Testament and Jewish tradition itself[10] do censure some of them, we must be careful not to condemn them all as spuriously devout hypocrites.[11] Nor must we forget that the Pharisee movement was not homogeneous from the time of the Maccabees to that of 'Aqiba, for example, and that it had always embraced a great variety of trends, a fact which helps to explain the differences between those authors who have tried to define Pharisaism.

The Pharisee tradition mentions the famous "pair" of doctors of the Law, Hillel and Shammai, about the beginning of the Christian era (from about 30 B.C. to 10 A.D.).[12] Judaism owes its astonishing survival to the various Pharisee schools, the members of which were sedulously alert to keep themselves apart from those who did not practice the prescriptions of the Law (*'am ha-areṣ* [the "people of the land"]) and who were therefore "unclean." This may have caused the Pharisees to disdain the common herd (Jn 7:49).

2. The Sadducees

The history of this group is very involved. They can be considered as the descendants of the priestly and aristocratic classes of the Maccabean era, open to Hellenism and always ready to collaborate with those in power, whoever they were. They were conservatives so far as religion was concerned, whereas the Pharisees were rather progressive in comparison. They held to Scripture alone, rejecting the authority of the scribes' oral tradition and the obligation to accept new beliefs, such as the existence of angels, the doctrines of retribution and resurrection after death and, in general, the contents of the apocalyptic and messianic speculations (see Acts 23:8). But the sources from which we draw our knowledge of the Sadducees are all biased, so that we are in fact badly informed about them. However, we do know that most of them were priests, and that they apparently ceased to exist as a group after 70 A.D. Yet it is possible that in 135 B.C., under John Hyrcanus I, a group of priests had left Jerusalem and settled in the wilderness so that they could remain faithful to their beliefs. These, perhaps, were the Zadokites, or *Benê Sadoq,* of Qumran [where parts of a document known as the *Damascus Covenant* or the *Zadokite Work(s)* were found].

3. The Essenes and the Sectarians of Qumran

According to J. T. Milik,[13] there were four groups of Essenes: first, those who lived at Qumran in a kind of motherhouse conducted according to the *Manual of Discipline;* second, those who lived in camps in the region of Damascus;[14] third, those who were scattered throughout the villages of Palestine;[15] and, finally, the Therapeutae of Egypt. However, the trends in the sect varied from time to time. Although they lived on the edge of society and were separated from worship at the Temple, they were able to exert a certain amount of influence through those of their members who lived outside the community. The excavations at Qumran have provided ample documentation to show that they were part of a vast baptist movement.

4. The Zealots

Josephus describes these as a separate sect whose connections with the Sicarii are not very clear.[16] [The Sicarii were nationalists dedicated to the quiet removal of political opponents by secret assassination.] The Zealots were above all a resistance movement against Rome, dating back to the revolt of Judas the Galilean (Acts 5:37) against the census imposed in 6 A.D.[17] They have been variously regarded as being linked with the Sadducees, the Pharisees or even the Essenes. In any case, their role in the war of 66-73 A.D. was a decisive one. We find Simon the Zealot among the apostles chosen by Christ (Lk 6:15), and attempts have been made to explain Christ's death and the origins of the Church in terms of Zealotism. However, as opposed to the Zealot teachings, Jesus affirmed that the kingdom of God would come unawares (Mk 4:26-29) and that His followers were to "render to Caesar the things that are Caesar's" (Mk 12:17).

5. Other Groups

Besides the Pharisees, the Sadducees, the Essenes and the Zealots, about which literary sources inform us in varying degrees, there were other elements which went to make up the Palestinian world and the multifaceted Judaism of the first century A.D.

The relationship between Jews and *Samaritans* had deteriorated from the time of Nehemiah, passing through various stages marked by the destruction of Samaria by Alexander in 332 B.C. and of the sanctuary at Garizim by John Hyrcanus about 108 B.C., until a complete break occurred.[18] However, as a result of the discoveries at Qumran, the problem of the relationships of the Samaritans with the Jews must be viewed in a new light.

One group among the Jews themselves deserves mention,

namely, that of the *'ammê ha-areṣ*. The term *'am ha-areṣ* was first used to designate the mass of the people as opposed to those governing them, but it ended by meaning those who were ignorant of the Law and whose fidelity to the prescriptions on tithing and purifications was doubtful [see Jn 7:49].[19]

A place apart should also perhaps be given to the *Galileans*, whose recent (first century B.C.) "Judaism," remote geographical location and composite character clearly marked them off from other Jews; and the same may also be said of the *Hellenists* of the New Testament.[20]

6. Reciprocal Influences

Mention of the Hellenists brings up the far-reaching question of the Hellenization of Palestine in the first century[21] and of the relationships between the Diaspora and the Jews who lived in Palestine, relationships which were much closer than was formerly believed.[22] Here reciprocal influences were at work. The synagogues in Palestine clearly showed the influence of Greek culture, as did the teaching of the rabbis. On the other hand, many Palestinian traditions can still be detected in Hellenistic literature; and the Jews of the Diaspora accepted Aquila's literal translation of the Old Testament in place of the Septuagint—facts which prove that Jerusalem was still the center of the Jewish religion. Moreover, excavations in Israel have shown that, during the first century, religious life in Jerusalem was intense and even rigidly sectarian. Thus, for example, no samples of pictorial art were found there such as were discovered in abundance at Beth Shearim. Here we find a type of Judaism which is very different from that of the era of the Mishnah.

7. Gnosticism

We must remember, too, that the problem of Gnosticism occurred in ancient Judaism, as recent research has shown.

8. Primitive Christianity

Primitive Christianity must be viewed against this extremely complex background. At first, Christianity was just one religious movement among many others, preserving the basic elements of its origin, and—in the Judeo-Christian communities—even maintaining typically Jewish beliefs and practices, as is evident from an abundant literature. Christianity must be mentioned because it was partly in opposition to it that normative Judaism was formed. Although many attempts have been made to associate Jesus of Nazareth with one or other of the movements described above, none of them has been very convincing.

D. Rabbinical Judaism

The whole political and religious fabric of Judaism was shaken by the catastrophe of 70 A.D., and if it was to survive, its structures had to be entirely rethought. This was to be the task of Hillelite [more lenient] Pharisaism under Johanan ben Zakkai, who founded the academy of Jamnia (Jabneh) after escaping from Jerusalem. The Sanhedrin was set up again, composed of scribes and doctors of the Law, and the work of codifying oral tradition was begun.[23]

Judaism then took on an appearance so characteristic that authors have asked themselves if there really was any true continuity with the preceding era.[24] It is difficult to deny that such a continuity did exist even though Judaism began to assume a more monolithic aspect which allowed it to define itself clearly as against the trends which a short while before had existed in it. In fact, of all the sects and movements which had formerly flourished in Judaism, only one, that of the Pharisees, was able to survive. The reorganization done by Johanan ben Zakkai and the first of the *Tanna'îm* [that is, the rabbinic teachers of the period 20-200 A.D.] was strong enough to enable rabbinic activity to continue even after the catastrophe of 135 A.D. This activity moved to Galilee, centering on Tiberias, and continued to develop until 425 A.D.[25] But, in the end, it was to the schools of Babylonia that Judaism was to be indebted for the great "official" texts, such as the Targum and the Talmud, which gained recognition everywhere, even in Palestine, from the tenth century onwards.[26]

Chapter II

Relationships with God

by Annie Jaubert

Early Judaism was deeply rooted in the religious traditions of Israel and was nourished from the same soil. However, in the course of time, some of these traditions deepened, others were changed, and trends that had once been only possibilities later emerged into the full light of day. In this chapter and the next two, we shall examine the religious life of Judaism in its relationships with God and man, devoting a special chapter to worship and religious practices. These distinctions are necessary even though we are fully aware of their artificial nature, as we are of the inevitable limitations of so short a study as this.

A. The Covenant

Traditionally, God's relationship with His chosen people was that of a mutual agreement, a contract, a covenant. The Bible traces this covenant back to God's selecting the patriarchs Abraham, Isaac and Jacob at the beginning of the Jewish race (Gn 12:1; 15:18; 22:17; 26:3; 28:13). God's promise was irrevocable; He had entered into an eternal alliance with the fathers of the race, a covenant which He would remember forever (Ps 105:6-15; 42). This was to be Israel's basic reason for hope in distress (Ex 2:24) or in sin (Ps 106:

45). The prophets described the alliance between God and Israel in terms of marriage (Hos 1-2; Ez 16).

This alliance was based on a contract. God pledged His word to Israel, while Israel, in her turn, pledged herself to practice the Law, that is, to be a people "holy to the Lord" (Dt 26:16-19). The alliance had been sealed with the blood of victims at Sinai, with Moses acting as intermediary (Ex 24:5-6); and it would be perilous for Israel if she broke the oaths she had sworn (Dt 28-30; Lv 26). Yet God would always forgive her (Neh 9:5-35) and would never withdraw His love from His people (Is 54:6-10). At the end of time, she, His spouse, will become faithful; and the new Jerusalem is compared to a bride adorned in all her jewels (Is 61:10). For "the days are coming" when God "will make a new covenant with the house of Israel," when He will write His law "upon their hearts" (Jer 31:31-33).

A. Neher emphasizes the fact that the election of Israel is only one aspect of the election of all mankind.[1] In the priestly tradition [in the Pentateuch], God's relationships with humanity as a whole are reflected in His alliance with Noah (Gn 9:8-17).[2]

The characteristics of the biblical alliance are found vividly delineated in ancient Judaism. The *election* of Israel from among all the nations of the earth is expressed in various literary forms. "He appointed a ruler for every nation, but Israel is the Lord's own portion" (Sir 17:17). Divine Wisdom, coming "forth from the mouth of the Most High," and hence identified with the Logos, "covered the earth, . . . seeking a resting place." The Creator pitched His tent in the Holy City of Jerusalem, whence Wisdom spread out the magnificence of her gifts (Sir 24). In a very different allegory, in which men are represented by animals, the *Book of Enoch* relates the history of the world and tells how, from the midst of universal corruption, Noah, Abraham and Isaac emerge like white bulls.[3] The *Book of Jubilees* (pre-Essenian) enlarged on the pessimistic view of history. According to it, the world was given over to the temptation of the devils after the Flood,[4] but God Himself watched over Israel as its guide and protector.[5] He caused the holy seed of Jacob to spring forth, for the father of the Twelve Tribes was the plant of justice that was raised up for generations without end.[6]

In moving, poetic words, the *Fourth Book of Esdras* sang about Israel's election: "O Lord Most High! From among all the trees of the earth, you have chosen a vine! From among all that sprouts from the soil, you have taken a twig. . . . From among all the countries of the world, you have chosen a land; from among all the cities of men, you have sanctified a city for yourself; from among all the birds of creation, you have called a dove."[7]

Pseudo-Philo's *Biblical Antiquities* represented Israel under the traditional image of the vine cherished and cultivated by God and becoming the cosmic vine, a holy tree which reaches down to the depths and soars up as far as the throne of God.[8]

In short, Israel was the axis about which the world revolved. It was even said that the world itself had been created for Israel.[9] If, therefore, Jerusalem was punished and destroyed, would not the whole world return to the primordial chaos?[10] The ambiguity of the doctrine of Israel's election is accentuated as regards the Bible. Is the Bible a gift to all men or a national privilege? The same ambiguity is seen as regards the Law.

B. The Law

The Law was the pride of Israel, for it was the Law that distinguished her from other peoples. To the Israelite alone, says the *Book of Jubilees,* was given the task of keeping and sanctifying the Sabbath along with the holy angels.[11] "Well-beloved are the Israelites, for they are the sons of God. They have received the instrument by which the world was created," that is, the Torah.[12] A persistent legend, which may be very ancient, praised Israel for having chosen and accepted the Law that God offered her, whereas other peoples had rejected it.

For the sectarians of Qumran, and in the *Book of Jubilees,* the covenant with God was the most important thing, no doubt because of the prominence given to the renewals of that covenant. On the contrary, however, Orthodox Judaism, or at least the Judaism of the Pharisees, insisted less on the doctrine of the covenant than on the observance of the Law. This was a change of emphasis, and the religion of the covenant tended to become the religion of the Law. Faithfulness to God was measured by fidelity to the Law, and there were trends towards a theology of merit, of the value of good works.

To appreciate these ideas, we must first realize the demands which fidelity to the Law made on the "pious." At the time of the Maccabees, when part of the nation and most of the priests had allowed themselves to be won over by Hellenism, a large number of Jews were butchered for refusing to disobey the commandments of the Law (1 Mc 1:57-63; 2 Mc 6:8-7: 42). When Pontius Pilate was governor, the Jews refused to allow the Roman standards to be brought into Jerusalem because they bore the image of Caesar; and when they were threatened, they declared that they were ready to die rather than break the Law.[13] In the same way, the Jews were the only ones in the Empire to rise up against Caligula when he had his statue placed in the temples. In this instance, too, they preferred to die rather than see the Roman Emperor's graven image in the Temple at Jerusalem.[14] Because of this tenacity of the Jews, the Romans had to give them special status in the Empire which would allow them to observe their Law. We can talk glibly about fanaticism, exaggerated nationalism, the intransigence of the Zealots who finally threw in their lot with the Sicarii, or the despair of the priests who cast themselves into the flames of the burning sanctuary;[15] yet who can estimate the part that true fidelity to the First Commandment played in all this?

The Pharisees have often been reproached for their casuistry, but such legalistic hair-splitting threatens every structured religious tradition. Too, over-diligence in religious observances can be the result of a sincere search for the will of God. Some *logia* [words of Christ] handed down in the Judeo-Christian atmosphere of St. Matthew's Gospel declare that not an iota of the Law will pass away and that whoever violates one of the least of the commandments shall be the least in the kingdom of Heaven (Mt 5:17-19). What Christ condemned was not the meticulous keeping of the Law but rather forgetfulness of the essential commandments of "justice, mercy and faith" (Mt 23:23), and especially the hypocrisy of certain teachers who "bind heavy burdens, hard to bear, and lay them on men's shoulders; but they themselves will not move them with their finger" (Mt 23:3-4).

Nevertheless, a morality in which the merit of good works plays a large part is not without its own dangers, as is illustrated in the parable of the Pharisee and the tax-collector (Lk 18: 10-14). Although certain passages in rabbinical texts recommend disinterestedness in the matter of reward for good works,[16] the whole trend of these texts is to show how important are the merits that can be acquired by the study and practice of the Law.[17] The author of the *Second Book of Baruch,* faced with the disaster of the destruction of Jerusalem, could no longer understand what was the use of the good actions accumulated by the just,[18] and he is more astonished at the inefficacy of good works than he is at the apparent failure of God's promises.

It is this type of mentality that was contrary to the spirit of the Gospels: "When you have done all that is commanded you, say, 'We are unworthy servants' " (Lk 17:10). This tendency to trust in the works of the Law drew an impassioned reaction from St. Paul (Rom 3:20-4:25; Gal 3:1-18). Yet we must be alert not to oversimplify matters even in the rabbinical tradition. Some of the most beautiful ancient prayers, such as those of the *Shema,* speak of the mercy, love and fidelity of God. In the *Shemoneh Esreh* ("the Eighteen Blessings"), there is a prayer for conversion: "Convert us to you, and we shall be converted. Renew our days as you did before. Blessed may you be, for you accept conversion. Forgive us, Father, for we have sinned against you. . . ." God was always ready to welcome sinners, while the just, those who were truly pious, knew that they were justified only through the mercy of God.

Attitudes towards merit, reward and freely-given mercy were therefore diverse in Jewish and rabbinical circles, and Philo of Alexandria confirmed this diversity in New Testament times.[19] But if one concentrates on unravelling collective as opposed to individual trends, there is no doubt that during this era it was the reform movements that placed the emphasis on Israel's sin and on the need for inner conversion on the part of the people of God.

C. Sin and Grace

The realization of sin and the need for expiation were traditional in Judaism, but in non-official circles, too, we find at least two movements based on the call to repentance: first, that of John the Baptist (Mk 1:4),[20] which Christ reiterated (Mk 1:15); and second, that of the sect at Qumran, which may have influenced John the Baptist's appeal. According to the ancient source common to both Matthew and Luke, John the Baptist held that even the title "son of Abraham," that is, appealing to the merits of one's ancestors or to fleshly inheritance, was of no value: "God is able from these stones (*'abanim*) to raise up children (*banim*) to Abraham" (Mt 3:9; Lk 3:8). Men had to flee from the anger that was to come, for the axe was being laid to the root of the tree. The Qumranians, too, demanded conversion of heart from those who wished to join their community and escape the coming extermination.[21] Conversion had to clear the way for the coming of God (Mk 1:3).[22]

The formula for confessing sins, "We have sinned, we and our fathers,"[23] was traditional in acknowledging the sins of the fathers as those of the sons, thus placing the accent on Israel's fundamental infidelity.[24]

The ritual at Qumran insisted on inner dispositions because no expiation or purification by water, no sea or river, but only the spirit of righteousness and humility could cleanse and soften the obdurate heart.[25] Nevertheless, the actual purification, which had to be continually recommenced, was not an end but a beginning. The great purification would come on the day of God's visitation, when all perversity would be abolished and the Spirit of truth would pour forth like a purifying spring.[26]

In short, the hope of salvation, which was expressed in various forms at Qumran, was essentially the same as that found in the prophets, namely, the hope that God and, more precisely, His Spirit, would come to renew men's hearts.

One of the most amazing discoveries in the Desert of Judah was the Qumranian theology of sin and grace as contained essentially in the *Hymns of Thanksgiving* and the last part of the *Manual of Discipline*. (It is not possible to harmonize all the documents found at Qumran.) In words that are even more dramatic than those of Job or the Psalms, the author of the *Hymns* expresses his acute awareness of man's sin: "How shall a man count his sins, and how shall he, perverse as he is, reply to the judgement of justice? It is you, the all-knowing God, to whom all works of justice and the secret of truth belong; but to the sons of men belong the furtherance of iniquity and the works of deceit."[27] Now, God purifies the perverse soul from great sin[28] by the abundance of His goodness and the greatness of His mercy.[29] To God alone belongs man's justice.[30] Did the sectarians at Qumran believe in predestination? Their dualism and their doctrine of the two spirits would seem to indicate that they did, but the matter is still being discussed.

There was, therefore, at Qumran a concept of justifying grace, which, however, was actually only a deepening or perhaps an offshoot of the traditional biblical teaching on the new heart that had been promised to man (Ez 36:25-29; Jer 31:33; see also Is 1:25-27; Jer 50:20; Mi 7:19; Zec 13:1). However, it is remarkable that the Qumranians considered justification as a gift already present. The discovery of the *Hymns of Thanksgiving* has modified the partial, oversimplified view which experts used to have of Jewish spirituality in Palestine at the beginning of the Christian era. Some authors reduced the Jewish problem to a narrow concept of righteousness through good works, interpreting Judaism in the light of the teaching of St. Paul in particular and of the New Testament in general, but forgetting the polemical nature of these sources. Yet St. Paul himself never denied that there were Jews who were spiritual and circumcised of heart (Rom 2:10.29).

But even before the discoveries at Qumran, we knew that the Old Testament, especially the Wisdom literature [that is, from Job through Sirach in the Bible], teaches the purifying, living action of God in men's hearts (see also Ps 51:12-31; Is 44:22), and that theologians had shown the development of this doctrine in Hellenistic Judaism. However, our principal sources are the Book of Wisdom and the writings of Philo of Alexandria. We don't hesitate to use Philo extensively because, despite his philosophical and allegorical approach, he is often a veritable mine of information about the common traditions of Judaism . The main difference between his writings and those found at Qumran is one of emphasis, for he is less pessimistic about the nature of man than were the Qumranians.

The Book of Wisdom throws into relief prevenient grace

(6:12 ff.) and to some extent allows mention of God's dwelling in the soul, since the Spirit of God and Wisdom live in the upright hearts which they instruct (1:1-7; see 9:17-18).

Although the symbolism which Philo uses may be confusing at first, he does propound a real theology of grace. The philosophy of the school of Alexandria taught that everything that exists in the world, in nature or in man, is a gift of God, to whom thanks must be rendered.[31] But Philo further insists on the fact that God wishes to confer on man even higher and greater gifts, those of virtue and perfection. That is why, in his writings, the Promised Land becomes the symbol of Divine Wisdom,[32] and Isaac, the son whom Abraham was granted, represents the perfect nature which God alone can beget.[33] Isaac is he whom no one needs to teach because his knowledge comes from God.

In Philo, the purification of the soul is most often presented as illumination. The word of God enters the soul, penetrates its most secret depths with its light, and makes it aware of its sinful thoughts and shameful actions.[34] This word is a clarifying, devouring yet saving presence which destroys in the soul thoughts contrary to religion and which brings sanctification to it.[35] The purifying value which Philo attributes to the word of God is noteworthy, and it is found also in the New Testament (Jn 15:3; Heb 4:12).

D. *Experiencing and Knowing God*

Hence Judaism expressed in various ways the doctrine of God's initiative in coming to man and transforming him within. In many cases it was a question, not only of the spiritual life, but also of mystical experiences. Naturally, to obtain knowledge of these intimate aspects of Jewish life, we must rely on the brief scattered documents at our disposal and on those writers or schools that had developed a language for describing their experiences. Of course, the simple recitation of the Psalms was a vivid and ever-accessible expression of supplication and praise, and, for many of the faithful, the Psalms were the foundation and support of a profound spiritual life. But here we are concerned only with those later developments which were the fruit of Judaism's achievements in its search for God.

[The first five books of the Old Testament—Genesis, Exodus, Leviticus, Numbers and Deuteronomy—were known as the Pentateuch, that is, "the Five Scrolls," or simply as the Torah, that is, "the Law."] Now, by ceaseless meditation on the Torah, Judaism developed a certain number of symbols and myths which nourished its religious life and which often served in later times as a vehicle for the infant Christian Church. The events of Genesis, Exodus and the wandering in the desert were read, reread, retold and commented on. The Israelites were accompanid by a well-rock that quenched their thirst and that was a figure of the Law, of wisdom, of God's continued presence with them. They ate manna, a figure of the word of God (Wis 16:26).[36] They "ate this manna and drank the water of the Well so that thus they might assimilate the Torah into their very bodies."[37] St. Paul was to say that "Our fathers . . . all ate the same supernatural food and all drank the same supernatural drink" (1 Cor 10:3-4). Hence they could eat and drink the word of God (see Jn 6), which was both nourishment and light (Wis 18:4).[38] Not only that, but the word of God was identified with wisdom, which had protected and guided humanity throughout its history (see Wis 10 ff.) and was "an initiate in the knowledge of God" (Wis 8:4).

In short, through meditation on the Torah, and undoubtedly influenced by surrounding cultures, the Judaism of Christ's day had personified some of the attributes of God. These attributes were, so to say, God's ways of approaching man which could be described and which still safeguarded His transcendence. The most important of these developments for the origins of Christianity were those concerning the Logos or Word, the *Memra* of Adonai ["the Word of the Lord"] in Palestinian Judaism. The Judaism of Syria also venerated the Word, if we are to judge by the Odes of Solomon, a Judeo-Christian composition, the basic material of which is certainly Jewish.[39] But it is in Philo especially that we find a theology of the Logos, often expressed in the categories of Hellenistic philosophy.

Under Stoic influence, the Torah could be identified with the natural law inherent in the world.[40] But, in general, Philo, who saw the wandering in the desert as an allegory of the soul's ascent to God, shows the Logos as being on the highest degree of the scale of God's powers, an intermediary between God and man.[41] Stage by stage, Israel, a symbol of the race of "seers" or of the higher part of the soul, raised itself up to the most holy Word.[42] Only exceptional beings were able to go beyond the Logos[43] and, like Moses, enter the pathless, formless darkness that surrounds the Existent; but when Moses sought to reach God, he "understood that God in Himself cannot be grasped, and he even saw that He is invisible."[44]

Philo thus furnishes a sort of treatise on contemplation or the stages of the spiritual life that was to have great influence on the Christian school of Alexandria, and on Origen in particular. But Philo represents only one, the most intellectual, of the sectors of the Jewish religious life of the beginning of the Christian era. How can one describe the most profound aspects of Jewish piety at this time? The prayer of praise was practiced everywhere in Judaism. Had not man been created in order to render glory to God and to lead the universe to Him (Sir 17:10)?[45] The hymns of joy found at Qumran ("I praise you, Adonai. . . .") are similar in structure to the one pronounced by Christ (Mt 11:25). Spiritual worship and inner sacrifice are documented both in Philo and in the writings at Qumran that we possess.[46] And it is impossible even to estimate the degree which the life of union with God reached among "the poor of Israel." "Pray to your Father *in secret*," the Gospel tells us (Mt 6:6).

Josephus reminds his readers that piety is the aim of all occupations in life.[47] Certainly, the inner personal religious life of individuals surpassed the life of outer worship; yet individual piety and community worship intermingled and nourished each other. Hence a study of Jewish liturgy will give us further insight into the piety of Israel.

Chapter III

Worship and Religious Practices

by Roger Le Déaut, C.S.Sp.

Israel's concept of the covenant and election, the presence of God and the part the Torah played in her religion influenced both the form of official worship and the conduct of each individual's daily life. Here we can only sketch briefly the principal manifestations of Jewish religious life, both communal and individual, and describe its characteristic traits, some of which were to develop greatly in later Judaism, as we shall see.

A. The Role of the Temple

Since we do not have the space here to follow in detail the development of worship in the Temple, we shall confine ourselves to recalling several significant attitudes towards the Temple in the ancient Jewish world.

The Temple of Solomon was the pride of Israel and, as worship became centralized in Jerusalem, it assumed a pre-eminent importance in Jewish piety (Pss 27:4; 42:5; 84; 122; 134). Its very presence seemed the surest protection for Israel and Jerusalem (Jer 7), and its destruction in 587 B.C. was a terrible trial for the Jewish faith. It was, in effect, the sign of God's presence (Dt 12:5; 1 Kgs 8; 9:3) and of Jerusalem's special election (Ps 68:17). Although the prophets condemned the abuses sometimes committed there, they maintained a positive attitude towards it. Thus Ezekiel made it an essential element of the restoration after the Exile (Ez 40:1-44:9), and the post-exilic prophets would not rest until the Temple should be rebuilt and worship restored there. But why did the Jewish people and their leaders seem to have accepted so easily the final destruction of the Temple in 70 A.D. and the cessation of sacrifice? And why were they content to substitute for sacrifice other forms of worship, such as prayer, fasting, works of charity, and the study of the Torah?[1] This apparent ease of acceptance has led authors to the conclusion that, for a long time before the destruction, the Temple had ceased to play its once-privileged role in the Jewish religion. Then, too, the desire for a more spiritual form of worship (especially among the Jews of the Diaspora); the prophets' remonstrations against a priesthood and a liturgy without soul or real devotion; and the role assumed by the synagogue and the teaching of the lay scribes were all factors that could have engendered a certain disaffection towards the Temple. However, the situation seems more complex than that.

It is true that, from Old Testament times, there was among the Jews a trend of thought maintaining that Yahweh did not need a material dwelling (2 Sm 7:5-7; Is 66:1-2), but it had negligible influence until the era of the New Testament.[2] It is possible also that there were differences of opinion on the very concept of the Temple. We do know that in some Jewish circles there were at least some reservations about the part to be played by the Temple. Thus the Essenes, while not rejecting sacrifices in principle, held themselves aloof from the Temple, which they regarded as being defiled by an illegitimate priesthood and in which, they maintained, the feasts were regulated by an heretical calendar.[3] But in all this they were simply postponing to the eschatological era a worship that had been unavoidably interrupted. Their deep concern for the Temple is confirmed by the considerations that fill almost half the *Temple Scroll* and by the lists of *Mishmarôth* (lists of the priestly classes for service) discovered at Qumran. It is probable that their meals, which were prepared by the priests and eaten in common and in religious silence, and which were accessible only after a period of probation, had, in their eyes, a sacrificial character. The same was true of the meals of the Therapeutae described by Philo.

The Qumranians were convinced that they were living a liturgy in communion with that of the angels, since the community itself was regarded as a real temple.[4] Similar ideas are present in the New Testament (e.g. 1 Pt 2:4-6). The deacon, Stephen, voiced one current of opinion opposed to the Temple worship, a trend that was undoubtedly of Hellenistic origin [when he said: "Yet the Most High does not dwell in houses made with hands; as the prophet says, . . . 'What house will you build for me?' says the Lord. . . ."] (Acts 7:48-50).[5] But Stephen's words, like those of Jesus Himself about the Temple, must be read in the light of contemporary trends of thought and with due regard for the various epochs of redaction, in which Christian attitudes towards Jewish institutions could have varied considerably.[6]

Nevertheless, while admitting the existence of some trends unfavorable to the Temple, we must recognize that the mass of the people remained very devoted to it and that it played a leading part in the Jewish piety of the first century.

The New Testament itself testifies to the admiration aroused by the imposing edifice built by Herod (Mk 13:1-2; Jn 2:20), an awe that echoes the unanimous Jewish tradition.[7] Jesus violently condemned the abuses against the holiness of the "house of prayer" (e.g. Mk 11:15-17), and His disciples could find no better formula to interpret His action than the psalmist's ardent cry for the rebuilding of the Temple: "Zeal for thy house will consume me" (Jn 2:17; Ps 69:9). It was the favorite gathering place for the first Christian community (Acts 2:46; 3:1), and even Paul did not hesitate to return there, arousing the fury of "all the city" when he was suspected of bringing Greeks into the Temple, thus "defiling this holy place" (Acts 21:26 ff). And does not the Epistle to the Hebrews testify in its own way to the attraction which the majestic liturgy of the Temple had for the Jews? This liturgy was described with complacent pride, not only by Sirach (50:11-21), but also by Philo[8] and the author of the *Letter of Aristeus.*[9] The repeated references to, and precise recollections of, the performance of the rites of the Temple found in the Mishnah[10] testify to the authors' nostalgia for the vanished sanctuary and to the profound interest which the Jews had in the liturgy carried out there.[11] However, these documents are of Pharisee origin. But it does seem that the glorification of the Torah in ancient Judaism did not lessen enthusiasm for worship. In fact, the Torah prescribed minute details of the liturgy; and later biblical piety saw nothing paradoxical in this (Tb 1:3-8; Sir 7:29-31; 35:1-10). On the other hand, the fact that authors such as Philo emphasized spiritual worship did not in any way imply a deprecation of the worship performed in Jerusalem. Despite his frequent allegories on the Temple and priesthood, Philo acknowledged that the sanctuary was of capital importance, even to the extent of making it the tangible counterpart of the temple of the universe.

The central position of the Temple during the era of Ezra and Nehemiah was retained under the Maccabees. Attachment to the sanctuary can be measured by the violence of the reaction that followed upon the profanation of December, 167 B.C. The first care of the victorious Maccabees was to purify the Temple and perform a solemn dedication, one which became an annual feast for all Judaism. The Second Book of Maccabees, which is a continuous exaltation of the Temple, was intended to reawaken interest in the fate of Yahweh's sanctuary among the Jews of Alexandria. According to the Torah, the Temple was the center of Jewish religious life, and attacking it meant striking at the very heart of Judaism. This explains the anger aroused by the assertions which Jesus or Stephen made about the Temple, whether these assertions were received as sheer calumnies or unpleasant truths. Jerusalem was "the metropolis of the whole Jewish nation"[12] because of the Temple there—"this place revered by the whole world"[13]—and because of "the altar venerated by all the Greeks and barbarians."[14] The misfortunes of the Holy City and the Temple recur frequently in Josephus' writings, as, for example, in the last words he attributes to Eleazar before the fall of Masada in 73 A.D.[15] The historian, however, was not merely indulging in rhetoric or nationalistic lamentations. The Jews' love for the Temple was first and foremost a matter of religion.

The pilgrimages helped to maintain the Temple,[16] and, despite the practical difficulties, the prescription of Deuteronomy (16:16) ["Three times a year all your males shall appear before the Lord your God. . . ."] was by no means a dead letter.[17] In addition, the Jews were bound to the Temple by the yearly tax of half a shekel to be paid by all males over the age of twenty, and by the tithes and offerings which the populace at large had to give to the Temple personnel.

The Old Testament concept of the Temple as the place of the divine Presence (*Shekinah*) was a truth of common faith (2 Mc 14:35).[18] Turning towards the Temple was turning towards the Lord,[19] and the custom of praying in the direction of Jerusalem (see 1 Kgs 8:44.48), as David did (1 Kgs 6:11), was to survive in Judaism. The Temple was the earthly equivalent of God's heavenly home, towards which all prayers rose.[20] The sanctity of the Temple was emphasized by the increasingly sacred character of the successive parts of the building leading in to the most sacred part of all, the Holy of Holies, which the High Priest alone could enter (and that only once a year) to make expiation for the people. The sacrificial ritual was considered a gift of God allowing reconciliation and the forgiveness of sins. There was always the danger that the material act of sacrifice would be regarded as an automatic, magical means of justification; yet the attention to minute detail required by the correct performance of the rites could also express and spring from real piety. However, in every case, the sacrifice had to be accompanied by a confession of faults and the willingness to make up for wrongs committed.

Besides the official sacrifies, such as the Tamid offered morning and evening for the people, popular devotion added so many private sacrifices that, on feast days especially, provision had to be made for a multitude of sacrificers.[21] Even in the middle of the civil war that preceded the arrival of Titus in Jerusalem, the sacrifices went on despite the projectiles launched against the Temple.[22] And during the siege itself, the people were bitterly disappointed because the perpetual sacrifice could not be offered.[23] Love of the Temple is shown in the heartrending laments for its disappearance which are found both in rabbinical writings[24] and in the apocrypha.[25] *M. Ta'anith*[26] explains that the words, "on the day of the gladness of his heart" (Ct 3:11), should be understood as referring to the building of the Temple (which it compares to the gift of the Torah!); and the treatise ends with this prayer: "May it be rebuilt quickly, in our day!" which had become the recurring theme of so many Jewish prayers.

The institution of the *ma'amad* involved the whole people in the Temple worship. The priests were divided into twenty-four groups (1 Chr 24:4), each of which in turn functioned in the Temple for a week. The *ma'amad* also included Levites and laymen delegated to represent the people. While the *ma'amadoth* were in Jerusalem, another delegation went four times a day to the local synagogue to pray and read the Scriptures at the same times as the sacrifices were being offered at the Temple.[27] Thus the liturgy of the synagogue followed the rhythm of the liturgy in Jerusalem (see Jdt 9:1), so that the entire population could plainly see that they were closely associated with the worship at the Temple. The very titles of the offices at the synagogue were designed to perpetuate those at the Temple. Hence we must not exaggerate the possible part played by the synagogue in accounting for a supposed disaffection for the Temple. Temple and synagogue complemented each other, and there were synagogues in Jerusalem (Acts 6:9; 24:12) and even in the Temple itself.[28]

We can conclude that the evolution of Jewish theology with regard to the importance of sacrificial worship was above all an adaptation to a concrete situation, an adaptation that was made all the easier by the fact that, even before the destruction of the Temple in 70 A.D., the teachings of the prophets (see Dn 3:38-41, in the Septuagint) were being followed in regard to interior dispositions, penance, conversion, prayer and charity. Thus for a long time before sacrifices ceased being offered, the essential parts of true religion were being practiced.[29]

The destruction of the Temple alone does not perhaps explain fully the cessation of sacrificial worship.[30] But be that as it may, although sacrifice was one of the three things upon which the world rested,[31] when it ceased to exist, Israel was able to take refuge in the practice of good works and the observance of the Torah, thus proving that the worship which had stopped was not the only or even the most important support of its religion.

B. The Feasts

While the worship at the Temple was centered on the Presence of God in the midst of His people, the great feasts of Israel had become, at the period under discussion, celebrations of His liberating interventions. The themes connected with these feasts had multiplied, while the eschatological and messianic character of some of the feasts had come to be emphasized more and more.

1. Annual Feasts

The most important of the "pilgrimage" feasts was the *Passover.*[32] The Targum of Pseudo-Jonathan (Ex 12:42) tells us that the Passover commemorates the creation, the sacrifice of Isaac, the first Passover in Egypt and, finally, the coming of the Messiah at the end of time.[33] The antiquity of this synthesis of the ancient themes of the Passover is proved by the parallel texts in Philo, the *Book of Jubilees,*[34] Josephus and Pseudo-Philo. The Paschal celebration, calling as it does for the recitation (*haggadah*) of the miracles which God worked on behalf of Israel, explains the development of the themes which are so prominent in the paschal theology of the New Testament. The foods eaten at the Paschal meal were used as the basis for an obligatory question-and-answer lesson and a moral instruction (see 1 Cor 5:6-8).

The part played by the Passover liberation in the Jewish faith is analogous to that which the Resurrection of Christ plays in Christianity. The night of the Passover was a sort of anniversary of the covenant (Wis 18:6), since God had announced the covenant beforehand to Abraham in a preparatory scene (Gn 15). Only those who had entered into the covenant by circumcision were allowed to celebrate this feast (Gn 17:13-14; Ex 12:44.48). The Passover celebrations mentioned in the Old Testament signify also a return to the covenant (2 Chr 30; 2 Kgs 23:21-23; Ezr 6:19-22).

There was a tendency to make this feast a celebration of all Yahweh's interventions on behalf of His people, and so this festival, which Josephus calls "the national feast,"[35] took on a very pronounced messianic character. It expressed in concrete fashion the solidarity of Israel down through the ages and reinforced the sense of national identity. As the ritual directed: "In every age, each one has the duty to regard himself as if he personally had come out of Egypt."[36] The rites were given, at least from the first century A.D. onwards, an eschatological and messianic interpretation (as early as Jer 38:8, in the Greek). The Passover meal anticipated the messianic feast and revived popular hopes: "It was in Nisan that they were freed; it will be in Nisan that they will be so again" was an axiom that had become a law.[37] And the Messiah was expected to come at midnight, a tradition which St. Jerome confirmed.[38] The remembrance of the sacrifice of Isaac (Gn 22), which Jewish liturgy would later transpose to the feasts of the New Year, added an important overtone to the Passover ideology since it became the classic example of the perfect sacrifice. Moreover, tradition identified Mount Moriah [the site of Isaac's sacrifice] with the hill upon which the Temple was built, thus adding even greater emphasis to the event (2 Chr 3:1).

According to some authors the Tamid [the daily or "perpetual" sacrifice] commemorated the Isaac episode.[39] The position occupied by the Pasch in Jewish and Christian spirituality needs treatment in greater depth, since "Christian spirituality and Jewish spirituality are both paschal in principle."[40]

The biblical name for *Pentecost* is "the feast of harvest" (Ex 23:16) or "the feast of weeks" (Ex 34:22). Due to a small vowel change, the term *shābu'ôth,* meaning "weeks," was interpreted in the sense of "oaths" when Pentecost became, in some circles, a feast of the renewal of the covenant. According to the *Book of Jubilees,* this feast was the occasion for the taking of solemn oaths,[41] and it was celebrated on the fifteenth day of the third month. The most ancient manuscript of the *Damascus Covenant* also gives the third month as the date for the ceremony of the renewal of the covenant.[42] There is no longer any doubt that the sectarians of Qumran preformed this ceremony on Pentecost day, and the *Manual of Discipline* even provides us with the formula they used.[43] Pentecost was also the greatest feast of the Therapeutae,[44] but we cannot be certain that they made it a feast of the covenant. Because the Chronicler gives the third month as the date for Asa's renewal of the covenant (2 Chr 15:10-15), it is possible that the link between Pentecost and Sinai may be an ancient tradition in Judaism as a whole. In rabbinical writings[45] and in the Samaritan tradition, Pentecost is the feast of the gift of the Torah, an association which was almost inevitable, since Exodus (19:1) gives the thrid month as the date of the Israelites' arrival in the desert of Sinai.

The detailed chronology found in the *Targum of Pseudo-Jonathan* puts the giving of the Law on the 6th of Siwan, the usual date according to the Pharisees' reckoning. We do not know if this dating is an ancient one, since it was unknown to Josephus and to Philo, who associates the giving of the Law with the feast of Trumpets (Nm 29:1-6); nor do we know if it casts any light on the account which the Acts of the Apostles (Acts 2) gives [of the coming of the Holy Spirit at the first Christian Pentecost]. In this account of Pentecost, the traditions linked with the giving of the Law are reversed, because the Christian Law is described as being proclaimed to every nation and in every tongue.

The exact date of Pentecost was a matter of controversy between Pharisees and Sadducees, who had different interpretations of the words: "You shall count from the morrow after the Sabbath" (Lv 23:15). The Pharisees, as did the Christians later, linked the Pasch and Pentecost closely together, prescribing that the offering of the first sheaf should be made on the very next day after the Pasch, and that Pentecost should mark the closing[46] of the fifty days of the Paschal season. The ancient priestly calendar used at Qumran, in which the feasts fell on the same day of the week each year, always had Pentecost fall on a Sunday. This custom was also known to the Samaritans and the Therapeutae, and no doubt there is a continuity between this tradition and the later Christian practice.

The feast of Tents ("huts" or "booths"; Lv 23:34; Dt 16:13) was also called "the feast of harvest" (Ex 23:16), or simply "the feast" (Ex 45:25; 1 Kgs 8:2.65). At first it represented an offering to God of the fruits of the soil after the harvest and grape-gathering. The use of the *lulab* (palm) and the *ethrog* (citron), and the requirement of living for seven days in a hut, indicate the agrarian origin of the feast (Is 1:8). But in Leviticus (23:43), we find that the feast has evolved and been given a historical connotation in the sense that it is meant to recall that God had the children of Israel dwell in huts when they came out of Egypt. The dedication of Solomon's Temple coincided with this feast (1 Kgs 8:65 f.), a fact which gave it a special relationship with the sanctuary, the place of God's presence and protection. According to the Targum, the huts were to be a reminder of the clouds that protected the Israelites during their wandering in the wilderness. Ezra (3:4) tells us that the repatriated Jews held the feast as soon as the altar was rebuilt and even before the foundations of the Temple had been laid, while Nehemiah (8:13-18) describes a celebration according to the ritual given in Leviticus (23:40-43), with daily reading of the Torah (see Dt 31:10).

This feast is mentioned several times in Josephus,[47] who calls it "the holiest and most important feast,"[48] and it is described in detail in *M. Sukkah,*[49] where comment is made upon certain very popular rites, such as the procession of the priests every morning to Siloe (see Jn 7:37), the singing of the *Hallel,* the procession around the altar and the lighting of the four large candlesticks in the Court of the Women (see Jn 8:12), illuminating the whole city.[50]

The rite of the water and the theme of light must have been inspired by Zechariah (Zec 14), who, moreover, allocates to the feast of Tents the great gathering together of all the families of the world at Jerusalem and the eschatological triumph of the Messiah. This shows the importance this feast has assumed from the end of the fourth century B.C. onwards, and also the universalist spirit of some trends in Judaism.[51] The messianic nature of the feast developed readily in this atmosphere.

It is not surprising that the coins struck by Bar Kochba were adorned with motifs inspired by this feast. In 1960, in the famous "Cave of the Letters" in the Wadi Habra at Qumran, there was discovered a letter from Kochba or one of his lieutenants commandeering citrons for the celebration of the feast of Tabernacles.

The feast must have been popular in all circles, because the *Book of Jubilees* refers to it and attributes its institution to Abraham in person.[52] It is interesting to study the remains of it in the Christian world, particularly because it is the only one of the three great ancient Jewish feasts to be retained in a different form.

Besides the three great "pilgrimage" feasts, we should mention two other celebrations introduced by Judaism: first, that of the *Dedication* (*Hanukhah*) in December, which was instituted after the victory of Judas Maccabeus in 164 B.C. (1 Mc 4; see Jn 10:22), and which Josephus calls "the feast of lights";[53] and second, that of *Purim*, which commemorates the deliverance related in the Book of Esther (see also 2 Mc 15: 36). These two feasts had a very pronounced nationalistic character, whereas the feasts of the *New Year* and *Atonement* tended to develop a sense of sin and conversion by recalling the judgment of God. The feasts of Hanukhah and Purim have their roots in the Old Testament, but their meaning became clear only during the post-biblical period. They are so important in later Jewish society that we shall discuss their spiritual significance later.

2. *Weekly Feast*

The biblical meaning of the *Sabbath* is given in Exodus (20: 11) as a remembrance of God's resting after the creation, and in Deuteronomy (5:15) as a memorial of liberation from Egypt, but it was to be considerably enriched in Judaism. Linked as it was with the history of salvation, and with the covenant, of which it was one of the elements (Ex 23:12; 34:21), the Sabbath became "a sign for ever" between Yahweh and the children of Isarel (Ex 31:17). Violation of the Sabbath was the expression of revolt against God (Ez 20:12-17) and finally one of the causes of the chastisements of the Exile (Neh 13:18). It is therefore not surprising that observing the Sabbath became the mark of Jewish fidelity (Neh 10:32). It assumed even greater importance after the destruction of the Temple and during the Exile, when the other celebrations were impossible. Under the Maccabees, the Jews preferred to allow themselves to be massacred rather than violate the Sabbath rest by defending themselves (1 Mc 2:32-38; 2 Mc 6: 11), and Josephus tells of a similar incident.[54]

Rules for the observance of the Sabbath became more and more detailed (see Is 58:13; Jer 17:21 f.), but it is interesting to note that, as Jewish thought evolved, some groups were to become much stricter than the casuistical Pharisees. The

Book of Jubilees forbade, under pain of death, the use of marriage, the kindling of fires and the preparation of food on the Sabbath.

The New Testament condemned certain strict interpretations of the law of the Sabbath (Mk 3:4; Lk 13:15; Mt 12:2) but not the Sabbath itself (Mt 24:20; Lk 4:16). The words of Mark ["The sabbath was made for man, not man for the sabbath" (2:27)] are found in equivalent terms in the *Mekhilta Ex.* (31:12-14).

The Sabbath was, above all, the consecration of time to God, and it was to be marked by joy. *Jubilees* also laid down the punishment of death for anyone who fasted on that day.[57] This rigorism, however, was intended primarily to stress the obligation of *celebrating* the Sabbath, which should be honored, first of all, by worship in the synagogue, according to Pseudo-Philo.[58]

C. The Liturgy of the Synagogue and Prayer

In its history and development, woship in the synagogue was closely connected with the Sabbath and was, in a way, an intermediary between the official worship in the Temple and private religious life. At a very early date, the liturgy of the synagogue consisted essentially of the reading of the Torah and the prophets (see Acts 13:15; Lk 4), following a cycle that was to become fixed only in the second and third centuries A.D., that is, a reading followed by a version in Aramaic (*targum*) and a homily (see Neh 8), in a framework of blessings and prayers.[59] From this we can deduce that the teachings of the prophets and the piety of the Psalms were the common denominator of the ancient Jewish religion. By this means there was also developed an intimate knowledge of the Torah, which was necessary for living in accordance with God's will at every moment of life, for "perfection" or "justice" consisted especially in obedience. Like the Jerusalem Talmud,[60] Josephus attributes to Moses the institution of Sabbath meetings "to hear the Law read and learn it exactly."[61] And he adds: "Among us, if you ask anyone to recite the laws, he will repeat them all with greater ease than he would his own name."[62] This perfect blend of teaching and worship gave Judaism a cohesion that explains its survival. Meetings were also held on Mondays and Thursdays.[63]

The synagogue was a place for teaching (Mt 13:54)[64] which became principally a house of prayer, first among the Diaspora (see Dn 13:28, in the Septuagint) and then, after 70 A.D., universally. It was called *proseuché* in Philo and *proseucha* in the Jewish inscriptions in Rome, a term which is verified in Juvenal.[65] The liturgy of the synagogue came spontaneously to replace the worship in the Temple, and the well-known text in Malachi (1:11) about the sacrifice that is offered everywhere to Yahweh becomes in the Targum: "Your *prayers* are a pure offering before me." However, the synagogue ritual was not fixed all at once but only by degrees.

Community prayer was stressed because God listens more willingly to the prayer of the community than to that of the individual.[66] Yet we must point out that the synagogue favored the development of personal prayer and provided admirable models thereof. The treatise *Berakhoth,* prescribing as it does prayers for every action and moment of life, proves the important role that personal piety played in Judaism. Like Jesus and St. Paul, the teachers of Israel inculcated the necessity of prayer. This is what is meant by "Love the Lord your God . . . with all your heart" (Dt 11:13). Prayer was a characteristic of the *saddiq,* the "just man," and is prominently mentioned in the deutero-canonical writings (Sirach; Judith; Esther, in Greek) and the apocrypha (the *Paralipomena of Jeremiah,* the *Psalms of Solomon*).[67]

Prayer and the study of the Torah could not be separated (see the second blessing in the *Shema*), and the very act of studying was itsef considered a form of prayer or worship.

Prayer was to be continual (Tb 4:19).[68] Daniel prayed "in the evening, in the morning and at noon" (Dn 6:11; see also Ps 55:18). The Mishnah imposed the recitation of the *Shema* (Dt 6:4-9; 11:13-21; Nm 15:41) in the morning and evening,[69] and that of the *Tefillah* (or "Eighteen Blessings") in the morning, afternoon (when the evening sacrifice was being offered in the Temple) and evening. These prayers are ancient (see, for the *Shema,* Mk 12:28),[70] but the elements of the *Tefillah* date only from between the pre-Maccabean period and the end of the first century A.D.

The doctors of the Law required that the prayers be recited, not as formulas, but as a real cry from the heart to God's mercy.[71] Although every prayer is answered, since prayer is stronger than chariots,[72] it is useless to multiply formulas (Sir 7:14; see also Mt 6:7-8)[73] or to accumulate titles for God, as seems to have been common in Hellenistic Judaism.[74] See the prayer of Eleazar in *3 Maccabees* (Chapter 6), a work full of examples of absolute faith in the power of prayer. The efficacy of prayer is, in fact, dependent on this faith[75] in a God who is infinitely near.[76] The Targum has preserved model prayers, such as that of Tamar (Gn 38:25) or those of Moses (Dt 32:50) and Abraham (Gn 22), in which confidence and faith are allied with the theme of merit.

Prayer was not divorced from effective charity. Cornelius, "who feared God, . . . gave alms liberally, . . . and prayed constantly to God" (Acts 10:2; see also *2 Enoch* 51:1.4). Charity and almsgiving played a large part in Jewish piety (Tb 4: 10 f.; 12:8 f.; Sir 35:1 f.). Even at Qumran, the ritual and liturgical prescriptions contained the commandment to show effective charity to one's neighbor.[77]

It was the custom to distribute alms on feast days (Jn 13: 29). There was a well-known list of works of mercy, such as consoling the afflicted, visiting the sick, burying the dead, which had to be practiced because God Himself had first given the example.[78] "Be merciful, even as your Father is merciful" (Lk 6:36) is a targumic paraphrase.[79]

During this period of the history of Judaism, the prayer of intercession was developed. It was first reserved to "official" intercessors, such as kings, priests and prophets, but it was later extended and became surrounded with a type of ritual. Expiation itself was regarded as an intercession.

While there were more or less traditional times for prayer, every important event was accompanied by prayer, so that religion suffused the whole of life—marriages, meals, deaths, entering and leaving the house, etc. We shall mention one more occasional celebration, namely, circumcision, because of the importance it had assumed in the Jewish religion. It became the sign of the covenant—Acts (7:8) speaks of "the covenant of circumcision"—and hence of Jewish identity (1 Mc 1:15. 49), which was to be defended even to death (2 Mc 6:10), and it was to take on an increasingly complex meaning. Thus the ancient commentators on Exodus 14 endowed it with a sacrificial and expiatory value.[80] The liberating blood of the Passover was to be associated with the blood of circumcision to demonstrated that men must take a personal part in their salvation.[81] The Targum (Gn 17:26) puts the circumcision of Abraham on the same date as the feast of the Passover.[82] In Jewish tradition, the expression "the blood of the covenant" came finally to be reserved for the blood of circumcision and, in Pseudo-Philo, the term "covenant" refers directly to the circumcision of the young Moses, which marked him as a Hebrew.[83]

D. Fasting and Asceticism

The later parts of the Old Testament place special emphasis on fasting (Is 56:6-8; Jl 2:12; Est 4:16), and the number of official fast days gradually increased (see Zec 7:5; 8:19). Fasting and abstinence, especially from meat and wine, were considered as normal elements in the life of anyone who wished to be pleasing to God. They were signs of penitence, ensured victory over sin, fostered prayer (Ezr 8:23; Neh 1:4; Dn 9:3; Bar 1:5; Tb 12:8; Jdt 8:5; 9:1), and prepared the soul to receive divine revelations (Ex 34:28; Dn 10:3.11; *4 Esdras* 5:13; 6:31; *Test. Ruben* 2:1; see also Lk 2:36-39). The characters in the apocrypha are usually champions of fasting,[84] as is evident from the *Testaments of the Twelve Patriarchs*.[85] The *Apocalypse of Elijah* condemned those false teachers who said that fasting had not been created by God.[86] The levite, Taxo, retired with his sons to a cave to fast for three days before going to his death rather than transgress the commandments of God. Fasting is often mentioned in the New Testament (Mt 4:2; Acts 13:3, etc.), which also testifies to its occurrence in Judaism (Mt 6:16; Mk 2:18; Lk 18:12). In pagan eyes, fasting seemed to be a characteristic trait of the Jews,[87] while the *Ta'anith* treatises in the Mishnah and Talmud contain very ancient references which corroborate those found in Jewish literature at the beginning of the Christian era.[88]

Asceticism was a much-debated problem in ancient Judaism,[89] so that the question arises: to what extent can asceticism be reconciled with Jewish theology? One author, W. D. Davies, says bluntly: "Asceticism . . . is largely alien to Judaism, and is condemned by the rabbis."[90]

But we should first of all define what "asceticism" means in the context of Judaism. The discoveries at Qumran have supplied the most abundant and explicit documentation on this subject, and hence it would be best to defer a detailed study of asceticism in Judaism until the texts have all been published. Was the asceticism practiced at Qumran a kind of pre-Christian asceticism, or was it instead a form of Greek asceticism as Philo or Josephus thought when they explained the retreat into the wilderness as a desire to escape the pollution of the city, and celibacy as a flight from jealousy about women? Or was it a form of extreme fidelity to the demands of purity [that is, *legal* purity] derived from the interpretation of Scripture, that is, from a *halakhah,* and based on the sectarians' conviction that they were the people of the new covenant and that they alone possessed the true priesthood and the only legitimate worship?[91]

A deeper study will allow us to judge if the frequently-made comparison with Christian monasticism is valid or not.[92] It is possible that we shall not find here any real exception to the fundamental principle of Jewish spirituality that all creatures are good (Gn 1:31) and hence are a means and an occasion for praising God. The Qumran texts will therefore have to be compared with analogous data from Jewish literature if we are to clarify the complex problem of asceticism in Judaism.

Chapter IV

Relationships with Men

by Annie Jaubert

A. The Brotherhood of the Israelites

Israel was the name of the people of the covenant which their ancestor Jacob-Israel had entered into with God. All the Israelites knew that they were the sons of Abraham, Isaac and Jacob. They were all brothers, as the Law said (see Ex 2:11; 4:18; Dt 1:16, etc.), not only because of their common, distant ancestor, but also in their fidelity to God. A text from Malachi expresses this conviction clearly: "Have we not all one father? Has not God created us? Why then are we faithless to one another, profaning the covenant of our fathers?" (Mal 2:10). Entering into the covenant with God and belonging to His people were one and the same thing; and to break the covenant was to betray one's brothers and fathers as well as God Himself.

The *Book of Jubilees* emphasized this by representing almost all the oaths of alliance exchanged btween God and men as taking place on the day of the feast of Weeks, which is the feast of the covenant, the feast of oaths. The Book of Wisdom, which very probably regards the Paschal meal in Egypt as a kind of covenant ritual, insists on the reciprocal obligations of the Hebrews: "The saints would share alike the same things, both blessings and dangers" (Wis 18:9). The relationship begotten between Jews by their belief in and obedience to the One God was the closest and strongest of bonds.

This is what Philo teaches when he alludes to Moses' throwing the blood of the covenant on the people (Ex 24): "Why does (Moses) say: 'Behold the blood of the *diathēkē* (covenant) which the Lord made with you in accordance with all these words'? Because blood is a sign of family relationship. Now, there are two kinds of relationship: that which exists between men and derives its origin from ancestors, and that which exists between souls and derives its origin from Wisdom. Moses is certainly not referring to the relationship that derives from ancestors, because that is found among animals as well as among men. He is, instead, referring to the other kind of relationship, that which derives from Wisdom. For Wisdom is the source of the words and laws which we accept voluntarily, the ones which the ancient teachings proclaimed and imparted to those who wished to learn those most necessary lessons, the spirit of concord and the spirit of community."[1]

The same doctrine is stated in the *Fourth Book of Maccabees*: the bond between the seven brothers was based less on their blood relationship than on their brotherhood in religion.[2] The words of Christ: "Whoever does the will of God is my brother, and sister, and mother" (Mk 3:35), found here a fertile soil prepared for them.

The demands of the brotherhood of the Israelites were formulated in the well-known commandment of Leviticus: "You shall love your neighbor as yourself" (19:18), the neighbor being primarily he who belongs to the same race. Everything was to be done to free a brother from slavery, a point upon which Leviticus (25:38-55) contrasts the status of the pagan with that of the Israelite. Nevertheless, as regards lending at interest, the law extended the privilege of brotherhood to guests or residents in the land of Israel (Lv 25:35-37); only to strangers was it permissible to lend money at interest (Dt 23: 20 f.).

In New Testament times, Judaism definitely connected the commandment to love God with that of love for neighbor. It was no anachronism on St. Luke's part to put in the mouth of a Jewish lawyer the double commandment of the Law: "You shall love the Lord your God with all your heart, and with all your soul, and with all your strength, and with all your mind; and your neighbor as yourself" (Lk 10:25-28), words which St. Mark (12:29) and St. Matthew (22:37-39) attribute to Christ Himself. But the big problem was to know who was one's neighbor.[3]

The great rabbi, Hillel, is said to have taught a Gentile the whole Law in a few words: "Do not do to your neighbor that which you would not wish him to do to you. That is the whole Law, and the rest is only a commentary on it,"[4] a negative form of the Golden Rule which had already appeared in Tobit (4: 15). The connection existing between the love of God and love of neighbor had its roots in biblical tradition, since God the Father commanded love of brother; and in some Jewish circles just before the beginning of the Christian era there was explicit mention of this fact.

Philo divided the Commandments into two classees. The first class contained the first five Commandments, which refer to God (and to parents, who are like God in that they bring children into existence); and the second class contained the last five Commandments.[5] Elsewhere he explained that piety (*eusebeia*) and the virtue of humanity (*philanthrôpia*) are twin sisters.[6] In the Palestinian tradition, the *Testaments of the Twelve Patriarchs* also linked the two commandments as twins.[7] It is true that these texts have been the subject of some controversy, but there does not seem to be sufficient reason to regard them all as Christian interpolations.

It is remarkable that the community at Qumran insisted on the prescriptions of Leviticus: "You shall not hate your brother in your heart, but you shall reason with your neighbor, lest you bear sin because of him. You shall not take vengeance or bear any grudge against the sons of your own people, but you shall love your neighbor as yourself" (Lv 19:17 f.). The *Manual of Discipline*[8] and the *Damascus Covenant*[9] repeat the need for fraternal correction and the prohibition against bearing a grudge. The procedure of reprimanding one's brother in the presence of witnesses before introducing the matter to the assembly was laid down in the *Manual of Discipline*[10] and the *Damascus Covenant*[11] before it was described in Matthew (18:16).

A passage from Sirach, in a section that lacks Hebrew parallels, explains that sins are remitted only to him who forgives his neighbor (Sir 28:2-7).[12] Here, too, the ground was prepared for the Gospel. It is also possible that the recommendations of the *Testament of Gad*[13] about hatred and *agapé* indicate a pre-Johannine climate.

As can be seen, the brotherhood of the Israelites was not simply an ethical system. It was based on religious principles and was apparently an internal necessity for the people of God. But because of schisms and divisions, the complete realization of the brotherhood of all Israelites seemed to be attainable only at the end of time. The prophets had promised again and again that the Jews would then be gathered together (see Is 56:8; Jer 31:14; Ez 34:13; 37:21, etc.). However, they did not predict just the physical return of the exiles but foretold a time when the Israelites would have but one heart (Ez 11:19; Jer 32:39), a renewed heart that could only be one that was united to God and neighbor. It is probable that the community in the Acts of the Apostles (4:32—"The company of those who believed were of one heart and soul") regarded itself as the fulfilment of the ideal that had been foreseen by the prophets.

A community of this kind could have resulted from putting into effect the prescriptions of the Qumran documents, in which the ideal of communion was of primary importance. The very word which they used for "community" (*yaḥad*), and which implies the idea of union, was completely characteristic of the sect. The members of the community entered it in order to be "united in the counsel of God"[14] and "united to the holy congregation."[15] They were an assembly of the elect to whom God had accorded "a share in the lot of the saints and with the sons of heaven."[16] They formed one liturgical assembly in communion with the angels.

This community regarded itself as the community of the last days, and to it were applied symbolisms such as that of the cosmic tree,[17] or that of the solidly based house in which truth, sanctity and perfection are gathered.[18] This community had to allow its members to pass successfully through the upheaval that opened up the future, to bear the messianic[19] birth pangs and to welcome the new times. Although it was conceived as a community of conversion, a sanctuary wihin Israel itself, it sometimes shows remarkable points of contact with the primitive Christian community.[20]

Yet the ideal of expiation that emerged at Qumran was deeply imbued with "levitical" holiness. The sectarians had great difficulty in welcoming pagan converts. In a general way, the Judaism of the New Testament era was divided between a sense of mission to the Gentiles and the necessity of preserving its own unity by erecting protective barriers around it. Hence the tensions and differing attitudes towards non-Jews.

B. Attitude Towards the Gentiles

It was a well-established tradition among the Jews that God had given them a privileged role to play in regard to the other nations of the world: "All the nations of the earth will be blessed in you" (Gn 12:2, in the Septuagint). Looking into the future, the prophets saw the Gentile nations going up to Jerusalem (Is 2:2-5; Mi 4:1-3; Zec 14:16-21); and the great gathering-in of the Diaspora would carry the pagans with it towards the Holy City (Is 60).

The apparently inexplicable dispersion of the Jews among the pagan nations would then be seen to have had a divine purpose. Since the Babylonian exile in the sixth century B.C., the Jews had been scattered among the pagans in order to lead them to the true God. Their task was to tell the Gentiles of "the marvelous works" of their God (Ps 96:3.10), singing about those works among the nations (Ps 101:4; 57:10) and inviting the whole world to thank Him (Ps 66:1; 67:4.6; 117): "Sing, you nations, with His people" (Dt 32:43, according to the Septuagint).

The pagans were invited to be converted (see Tb 13:8). Philo wrote a short treatise on *metanoia,* that is, on conversion or change of heart, with the Gentiles explicitly in mind.[21] The love story, *Joseph and Aseneth,* proposed the proselyte Aseneth as the exemplar of conversion to Judaism. The missionary zeal of the Jews was considerable: we have all read of the sometimes indiscreet ardor of the Pharisees (Mt 23:15).

Jewish tradition certainly recognized the greatness of men, of all men, since they are formed in the image of God,[22] and many Jews had to admire the moral superiority of certain pagans. Thus for Philo, real spiritual worship could be found even outside the boundaries of Israel.[23] But all this did not lessen Israel's deep faith in her own mission. Numerous texts show the Israelites' conviction that they were the guides and light of the pagan nations. In the Septuagint version (Is 42:1), Israel is the servant that had received the inspiration to carry justice to the nations. She was charged with passing on the Law, the light of the world (Wis 18:4). The *Letter of Aristeas* related how Jewish sages had been the counsellors of King Ptolemy II Philadelphus.[24] And St. Paul could write to the Jews in Rome: "You are sure that you are a guide to the blind, a light to those who are in darkness" (Rom 2:19).

In this context, the role of Moses was considerably enhanced, for he was regarded as the greatest of all legislators.

To prove this beyond a shadow of a doubt, a thesis was proposed that could not but succeed with Jews as well as with Christians, the thesis of the philosophers' "theft." According to this thesis, the Greek philosophers owed their greatness simply to the fact that they had seen how admirable were the constitution and law of Moses and had imitated or "stolen" it without publicly acknowledging its source.[25] In the tragic Ezekiel, Moses had received, as it were, kingship over everything and possessed knowledge of "what is, what was and what is to come."[26] Philo represented Moses as the spokesman who communicated the sacred mysteries to men[27] and the one who guided the servants of God through the heights of heaven.[28]

Israel, therefore, was conscious of being the mediator for the whole world. Hence it is not surprising to find that, in a way, Hellenistic Judaism believed that Israel was the priest for the whole world. It was already clear in the Book of Wisdom (18:24) that Aaron was the high priest of the universe, "for upon his long robe the whole world was depicted." Philo, however, is the best witness to this belief. According to him, Aaron was the priest of the cosmos:[29] "The high priest of the Jews caused prayers and thanksgiving to ascend on high, not only in the name of the race of men, but also in the name of all parts of nature, earth, water, air and fire, because he believed, as was indeed the case, that the cosmos was his true fatherland."[30] Now, for Philo, the priesthood of the whole nation preceded that of the high priest.[31] Israel was "the nation that had received priesthood and prophecy for the whole race of men."[32] "The Jewish nation is to the inhabited world what the priest is to the city."[33]

[Although Philo was from Alexandria,] it is probable that the Palestinian Jews believed as he did in this matter, because for them, too, Israel was certainly the only effective intercessor. Gentiles went up to Jerusalem for the feasts (see Jn 12:20; Acts 8:27); sacrifices were offered every day in the Temple of that city for the Roman Emperor; and pagans could have victims sacrificed there. Even further, there was a tradition that anyone, Jew or Gentile, who invoked the merits of the Fathers and especially of the Aqeda (the sacrifice of Isaac, "bound . . . upon the wood"—Gn 22:9) would surely be heard.[34]

Nevertheless, it may be asked how many Jews, especially in Palestine, were really open to accept what we can call the salvation of the Gentiles (see Lk 2:32). The doctrine of Israel's mediation for the rest of mankind could sometimes assume rather grim aspects. Thus in the Qumran documents, there is no doubt that the community did see itself as having a "sanctifying" role; but this sanctification was to be brought about by the extermination of sinners and hence of evil.[35] There was a religious basis for the holy war of the sons of light against the sons of darkness: and this was undoubtedly the theology of the Zealots, too. The words of the Gospel: "You have heard it said: 'You shall love your neighbor and hate your enemy,' " (Mt 5:43), had their exact counterpart in the *Manual of Discipline,*[36] the enemy naturally being represented by the sons of darkness. It is difficult to say how the great body of the Jewish people regarded the idea of a holy war. Some Jews, such as Josephus, who were very conscious of the power of Rome, certainly looked upon it as sheer madness. But Scripture seemed to predict it (Ez 38:14 ff.; Nm 24:17 ff.). Philo regretfully envisaged it and hoped instead that the nations could be converted by persuasion.[37]

These glimpses will give some idea of the complexities of the trend of Jewish attitudes towards the Gentiles. All the evidence points to an interaction between Israel's traditional teachings and her concrete situation in the midst of the pagan nations. Roman domination had helped to heighten the feeling of Jewish nationalism. The Jews living outside Palestine aroused ambivalent feelings in their pagan neighbors. The majesty of their religion attracted "those who feared God," but their manner of living caused mocking comment, made social life difficult (e.g. the Sabbath observance) and caused them to be judged antisocial, while their tenacity of belief and their influence aroused disquiet and hostility. Long before the destruction of Jerusalem in 70 A.D., there had been pogroms in Egypt and elsewhere against the Jews, and the fictional descriptions in Esther and the *Third Book of Maccabees* may reflect actual situations of persecution.[38] This state of tension created for the Jews of the Diaspora a kind of permanent consciousness of a tragic destiny that sometimes peeps through the texts, and the conviction that they had a privileged mission to accomplish. Although Israel was the first fruits of the human race,[39] she was still the orphan in the family of nations. Or else she was like the burning bush, engulfed in the flames of persecution but never consumed; the angel, symbol of God's presence, shone in the middle of the fire, whose flames only brought out the beauty of the bush.[40]

The immense Jewish effort, which came to a climax precisely in the first century of our era, furnished the seedbed in which the young Christian Church took root and flourished. It was Christianity that gathered and preserved a large part of the Jewish heritage. It is noteworthy that Flavius Josephus, Philo and many apocryphal works have come down to us only through Christian hands. The spread of Christianity undoubtedly contributed to the later waning of Judaism, which, nevertheless, continued to pursue its own way, in argument or in dialogue, without ever losing faith in its own destiny.

Chapter V

Traditional Teaching

by Kurt Hruby*

Judaism was able to survive the two great national catastrophes, the destruction of the Temple in 70 A.D. and the collapse of Bar Kochba's revolt in 135 A.D., because of the traditional Pharisee-type teaching. It was this teaching which, in the midst of very severe trials, allowed Judaism to reach another dimension and evolve a new way of life. But this evolution could not have been accomplished without a long preparation, so that at a given moment in history, new institutions were ready to take over from the old ones that had lost their effectiveness. Thus it was that, first at Jabneh and then, after the great persecution unleashed in 135 A.D., at Usha and other places in Galilee, the Great Sanhedrin, which used to sit in the Temple itself, was replaced by the rabbinical sanhedrin, with, however, certain modifications demanded by the new political and religious situation. In the same way, the synagogue, which had existed for centuries side by side with the Temple, then began quite naturally to take care of the needs of worship.

By the time the Jews were able to return from the Babylonian exile, the groundwork for this evolution had been carefully laid. On the one hand, they had had to reorganize their whole

---

* Kurt Hruby is the author of Chapters V through X.

national and religious life to meet a situation that was completely different from that which had obtained before the Exile. According to rabbinical tradition, this reorganization and adaptation of life to new circumstances was the work of Esdras the priest and the *anshei knesset ha-gedolah,* that is, the assembly of scribes and doctors of the Law which he had gathered around him for that purpose,[1] and which handed down official doctrine as it was needed. On the other hand, the years of exile had also changed the people's attitude towards the Temple and the worship performed there. They had learned by harsh experience that the life of Israel could go on even though the Temple was no more. Furthermore, it is probable that the origins of what later became the synagogal system are to be sought in this period. The existence of an important Diaspora no doubt favored the evolution of such a system during the whole era of the second Temple [538 B.C. to 70 A.D.].

Thus, from the years 70 A.D. and 135 A.D., the academies and the synagogal system became the two centers of Jewish life and assured, not only the survival of Judaism, but also a considerable amount of development from the spiritual point of view. After the collapse of its ancient structures, Judaism was reorganized exclusively on the basis of the Torah and its traditional interpretation.

A. *Starting Point*

Rabbinical tradition teaches that there are two branches of revelation: the *written* Torah (*Torah she-bi-khetav*), set down in the Pentateuch; and the *oral* Torah (*Torah she-be'al peh*). These two branches of revelation are of equal right because they are of divine origin and were both revealed at the same time to Moses on Mount Sinai.

This basic traditional Jewish concept of revelation is expressed in the Midrash *Sifra on Leviticus*:

> These are the customs, rules and laws (*ha-ḥûquim, ha-mishpatim,* we-ha-torot) which the Lord established between Himself and the Israelites on the mountain of Sinai, with Moses acting as intermediary (Lv 26:46). *Ha-ḥûqim* are the *midrashot* ("interpretation"); *ha-mishpatim* are the *dinim* ("rules of law"); *ha-torot* (plural of "Torah")

> is that which teaches us that two Torahs were given to Israel on Sinai, one in writing and the other by word of mouth. . . ."On Mount Sinai, with Moses acting as intermediary," teaches us that the Torah was given to Moses on Sinai with (all the) *Halakhot* ("rules of application") and all the details that relate to them (*diqdûqeihem*), as well as all the interpretations (*pérûshim*).[2]

The etymological meaning of the word "Torah" is "teaching" or "instruction." By His gift of the Torah, God ratified the covenant He had made with His people. In the Torah, too, He showed them how they were to follow their vocation as the witness among the nations to Him, the One God who had mercifully bent down to the human condition and had revealed Himself to mankind by means of the people whom He had chosen from among all the nations of the earth and whom He had made the privileged instrument of His plan of salvation.

In this sense, the Torah is "the book of the covenant" (*séfer ha-berith;* Ex 24:7). It is the precious pledge given by a God who, by His very Nature, is "the faithful God who keeps covenant and steadfast love with those who love him and keep his commandments" (Dt 7:9). By this covenant, the people of God had become the Lord's heritage (*yerûshah;* Dt 2:12) and patrimony (*naḥalah;* Dt 9:25, etc.), and, in return, they were to prove their devotion to Him by unconditional fidelity to His will as expressed in the *miṣwoth,* the commandments of the Torah. Thus the Torah is also, but not primarily, a norm of action and conduct, and hence a *code of law.*

Like every other code of this kind, the Torah contains a group of rules which are often couched in general terms. To ensure the concrete application of these rules in everyday life, and, more especially, to allow them to be adapted to situations that are constantly changing and often very different from those envisaged by the code, a certain "first interpretation" must coexist, as it were, with the code. This state of affairs was foreseen by the Torah: in case of difficulty in matters of law, the Jews were to consult "the Levitical priests, and . . . the judge who is in office, . . . and they shall declare to you the decision" (Dt 17:9 ff.). Originally, the oral Torah was simply this first interpretation, indispensable to the written Torah.

N.B.

B. Contents of Tradition

According to rabbinical tradition, the written Torah already contained within itself a complete divine revelation. Thus the doctors of the Law could say that the rest of revelation, contained in the other books of the Bible, was needed only because Israel was incapable of extracting all the riches already present in the Torah. On this subject, the Midrash says: "If Israel had been worthy (of the Torah), the revelation contained in the prophetical books and the Writings would have been unnecessary."[3] Because of the basic nature of the Torah as revelation *par excellence,* the Prophets and the Writings of themselves contain nothing that is not already in the Torah in one way or another, at least implicitly. It can be said, therefore, that everything the prophets were to teach had already been revealed on Sinai.[4] Using this principle, the whole of Sacred Scripture is sometimes called simply "the Torah." To distinguish them from the Torah proper, the prophetical books and the Writings are called *qabbalah,* "tradition," for they are the first interpretation of the Torah *be-ruaḥ ha-qodesh,* that is, by the intervention of the Holy Spirit.

The *Tanakh,* that is, divinely inspired Scripture, is holy and normative and is made up of the *Torah,* the *Neviim* or prophetical books, and the *Ketûbim* or Writings. (The word *Tanakh* is formed from the initial letters of the three words). Scripture is the norm and source of all teaching: it is *miqra,* "that which must be read"; and that is why all instruction must be based on Scripture and rooted in it.

The Talmud would later specify in even greater detail the nature and contents of the revelation on Sinai. We read in the treatise *Berakhoth*:

> Why is it written: "The Lord said to Moses, 'Come up to me on the mountain, and wait there; and I will give you the tables of stone, with the law and the commandment (*ha-Torah uve-ha-mitzvah*), which I have written for their instruction' " (Ex 24:12)? "The tables," that is, the Ten Commandments; "the law," that is, the Scripture (*miqra,* in the sense of "the Pentateuch"); "the commandment," that is, the Mishnah; "which I have written (*ash-*

> *er katavti*)," that is, the Prophets and the Writings (*ketûbim*); "for their instruction," that is, the Gemara. This teaches us that all those things were given to Moses on Sinai.[5]

The Jerusalem Talmud goes even further:

> "And the Lord gave me the two tables of stone written with the finger of God, and on them were all the words (*kol ha-devarim*) which the Lord had spoken with you on the mountain. . . ." (Dt 9:10). (This means) absolutely everything (*kol ba-kol*)—Scripture, Mishnah, Talmud, and Haggadah, and even what a clever pupil (*talmid watiq*) will point out some day in his teacher's presence—all that has already been given to Moses on Sinai.[6]

The oral Torah, just like the written one, comes from God and was handed down from generation to generation by the "links of tradition (*shalshelet ha-qabbaḷah*)."[7] The contents of the whole of tradition is called *midrashoth* ("inquiries," "interpretations") in the rabbinical documents. Thus the Midrash, in the primitive meaning of the term, which comes from the verb root *d-r-sh* ("to scrutinize," "to examine closely"), is the most ancient form of scriptural interpretation.

In the opinion of the doctors, the oral Torah has not been preserved in all its purity, and so it must be renewed with each generation. It is possible to do this because, in a way, the oral Torah is contained in the written one and can be "recovered" therefrom.

C. The Need for Interpreting Scripture

Although the rich contents of divinely inspired Scripture are inexhaustible, they are available only to those who know how to interpret them. In Scripture, God does not speak as men do but expresses Himself in such a manner that His words may be understood in different ways.

In the Midrash *Shir R.* on Cant 1:2, the vast treasures of Scripture are described in a parable:

> R. Eli'ezer (b. Hyrkanos) says: "If all the oceans (of the world) were of ink, if all the reeds were pens, if the

> heavens and the earth were rolls (of parchment), and if all men were scribes, then even all that would not be sufficient to write down all the words of the Torah that I have learned (from my teachers), although what I have received is comparable to the amount of water taken up by a man who dips the tip of his pen in the sea."

In order to understand the Torah thoroughly, one must know the rules of interpretation. Everything in Scripture is of divine origin, nothing is there by chance, and even what appears to be the most insignificant detail has a profound meaning.

If the Torah is to be truly a rule of life for the community, it must be interpreted authentically, for only then does it become normative. Without this interpretation, the text of Scripture would not have binding force. Down through the centuries, such interpretation has been the task of the teachers of tradition, and it is they who give the *pérûsh,* the meaning of Scripture.

The Mishnah, therefore, is the reappraisal of the legislation of the Torah in the light of tradition. However, the Mishnah is not regarded merely as a supplement to the Torah but is seen to have been necessary from the beginning because of the very nature of the Torah. The Mishnah is therefore an authentic branch of revelation.

This interpretation of Scripture is divided into two great categories, the *Halakhah* or normative interpretation, and the *Haggadah* (or *Aggadah*), the narrative and allegorical interpretation. In rabbinical literature, the *Halakhoth* [plural of *Halakhah*] are also often called *middoth* ("standards," or "rules"). A *Halakhah* is, by definition, a normative tradition based on the divine teaching contained in Scripture and therefore clothed with God's authority. There are a certain number of ancient *Halakhoth* which cannot be linked directly to a passage in Scripture, and in tradition these are called individually *Halakhah le-Mosheh mi-Sinaï,* that is, a *Halakhah* revealed directly to Moses on Sinai.

The *Haggadah,* on the contrary, is the free and often allegorical interpretation of a scriptural text and is not normative in character. This, too, is held to have been partly forgotten; hence it must be reconstituted with the help of the rules for the interpretation of Scripture, of which rabbinical literature recognizes seven, by extension thirteen and even, in their most developed form, as many as thirty-two. These rules, too, are called *middoth.*

The *Halakhah* and *Haggadah* are derived, by deduction, from the Torah, which thus appears as the true source of all instruction. According to the Midrash, God had given Israel the written Torah in an allusory form (*remez*), with the result that its contents were incomprehensible by themselves:[8] but He had explained it in the oral Torah. Hence the written Torah contains the *kelal* ("general principle"), while the oral Torah contains the *peraṭ* ("detail").

Tradition also distinguishes between those *Halakhoth* which are *mi-de-oraïta,* based directly on a principle laid down in the Torah, and those which are *mi-de-rabbanan,* the result of scholarly deduction. But this distinction does not affect in any way their binding power in regard to religious practice.

One of the greatest differences between the two branches of revelation is that the written Torah was given once and for all time, while the oral Torah is never finished, since the work of interpreting and applying the written Torah to current conditions is the duty of the teachers of traditional instruction in every generation.

D. *The Relationships Between the Two Branches of Revelation*

The written Torah is superior in dignity to the oral Torah, but from the point of view of application to concrete circumstances, the decisions of the oral Torah must always be followed.

The Midrash explains the matter as follows:

> Pay more heed to the words of the scribes (*soférim,* which means the same as *hakhamim,* "wise men," "teachers") than to those of the Torah; for that is what is said (Cant 1:2): "For your love is better than wine": the words of the well-beloved ones (the teachers of tradition) are better than the wine of the Torah. Why? A halakhic teaching cannot be correctly deduced from the (bare words of the) Torah, which is tightly sealed and consists

> entirely of allusions. . . . (On the other hand,) by using the words of the teachers as a point of departure, one can deduce rules properly-so-called (from the Scripture text) because it is they (the teachers) who interpret the Torah.[9]

In *M. Soférim,*[10] the Torah is compared to water, the Mishnah to wine, and the Gemara to spiced wine: it is due to the teachers' instructions that one is in a position to carry out the precepts of the Torah correctly.

For these reasons, the oral Torah must be studied in preference to the written one, as the Talmud says:

> (As regards) those who busy themselves exclusively with Scripture, that is a way of studying that is not study at all. (As for) those who occupy themselves with the Mishnah, that is a (true) way to study; it earns both results and reward. (As regards) those who devote themselves to the Gemara, there does not exist a better way to study![11]

E. Method of Handing Down Tradition

The tradition elaborated in this way was gradually codified in the major documents of rabbinical literature—Mishnah, Tosefta, Gemara (Talmud) and Midrashim. (See below, Appendix: Sources.) Of course, setting down the oral tradition in writing was really straining the basic principle of the oral Torah and hence of the essentially oral transmission of this inheritance. Nevertheless, there were two good reasons for resigning oneself to doing so. On the one hand, the amount of material accumulated over many generations had become so vast that, in practice, it was impossible to retain it all by sheer memorization. On the other hand, and this was the main reason, the weight of events was such that notable parts of this tradition were in danger of being irretrievably lost. At the time of the persecution unleashed by Hadrian after 135 A.D., Roman law forbade the teaching of the Torah, and numerous doctors, the most prominent of whom was R. Aqiba b. Joseph, died as martyrs, either because they had taken an active part in the insurrection, or because they refused to obey the new law.

In turn, the Mishnah and its contents came to be discussed and refined in the academies of Palestine and Babylonia by the *Amoraïm,* a name given to the teachers of the post-Mishnaic era (from the third century A.D. on). The results of these discussions were set down in the two Talmuds, the Palestinian (or Jerusalem) and the Babylonian. The compilation of the Jerusalem Talmud was completed towards the end of the sixth century and that of the Babylonian Talmud about a century later.

Although the prestige of the Palestinian schools remained very high, nevertheless the intellectual center of Judaism shifted more and more towards Babylonia, where the most ancient Diaspora flourished and where life was much less disturbed by external events than in Palestine. Furthermore, it was in Babylonia that two academies were founded which, for many centuries, were to be the true centers of Jewish intellectual and spiritual life—the school of Sûra, founded in 219 A.D., and that of Pûmbeditha, founded about 250 A.D. Because of this situation, the authority of the Babylonian *Resh Galûta,* or Exilarch [the most important doctor of the Law in Babylonia], was often effectively greater than that of the Palestinian *Nassi,* or Patriarch. In Palestine, furthermore, the patriarchate was abolished in 425, under Theodosius II, and the academy of Tiberias, the seat of the patriarch, was closed. And the Babylonian Talmud alone is the source of rabbinical jurisprudence. The work of interpretation and codification of tradition continued in Babylonia during the whole period of the *Geonim* (heads of academies), whose teaching was normative for the whole of Judaism. The academy at Pûmbeditha continued its activities until about the middle of the eleventh century.

Another category of rabbinical literature contains the numerous homiletic Midrashim, which were based on homilies delivered in the synagogue.

Chapter VI

The Torah

A. The Gift of the Torah

"The Lord was pleased, for his righteousness' sake, to magnify his law (Torah) and make it glorious" (Is 42:21). Israel's very existence is based on the special relationship which God established between Himself and His people, and which He consecrated forever by His gift of the Torah. This idea is the core of the Jews' concept of their mission, a mission which rabbinical Judaism views in an essentially functional way. Israel's task is to act as the privileged witness to God's truth before the rest of the world. She will carry out that task by working out her own history, and, as the great prophets teach, she will thus bring all the nations of the earth to recognize the One God and, in their turn, to take upon themselves the *'ol malkûth shamayim,* the "yoke of the kingdom of God."

This is the great moment for which Israel prays in the beautiful *Aleinu* prayer, which is recited at the end of every service, and whose principal elements date back to the time of Rab (Abba Arikha, president of the academy at Sûra, who died in 247 A.D.):

> This is why we hope in you, Lord our God. (We hope) soon to see the splendor of your power. (We hope) that you will make idols disappear from the earth and that you will exterminate false gods, so as to set the universe

> right again by (the recognition of) the kingship of the Almighty, in order that all men will invoke your name and all the wicked peoples of the world will turn to you. Then all who dwell on earth will recognize and know that every knee must bend before you and and every tongue swear (by you). (See Is 45:23.) They will bend their knees and fall on their faces before you, rendering homage to the glory of your name. Then everyone will accept the yoke of your kingdom so that soon you will reign over them for evermore. For kingship is yours, and you will reign for evermore in glory, as it is written in the Torah: "The Lord will reign for ever and ever" (Ex 15:18). And it is also said: "And the Lord will become king over all the earth; on that day the Lord will be one and his name one" (Zach 14:9).

But that which was only a future prospect for the rest of humanity was a present reality for the Jewish people from the moment they accepted, once and for all, the *'ol malkûth shamayim* by receiving the Torah and the *miṣwoth,* the divine commandments contained therein. The Jewish people, collectively and unanimously, as the Midrash so vividly puts it, had made an act of confidence in God by replying, at the foot of Mount Sinai: "All that the Lord has spoken we will do, and we will be obedient" (Ex 24:7). The Jews had thus entered directly into the era of a salvation which from then on was offered both to the people as a whole and to the individual members. This salvation was offered in the Torah and by means of the Torah, the divine path that God had traced out for His own people. There was no question here of legalism or ultra-nationalism but of a way of life which is permanent sanctification and hence salvation.

Judaism has a very deep sense of sin, but it never developed a doctrine of original sin, as Christianity did. In Jewish eyes, sin is always an act of disobedience to God, a concrete act of defiance to a divine will which, thanks to the Torah, is known perfectly. Thus forgiveness can be obtained only through a deliberate act of *teshûvah,* of returning to God by obedience to the Torah. In Scripture, God warns of the consequences should the whole people or an individual depart from the Torah and its precepts. (See in Lv 26 and Dt 28-29 the wonderful promises of blessings for fidelity to God and the terrible curses for betraying Him.) Nevertheless, the Torah is still the supreme criterion and the permanent point of reference: "If you walk in my statutes and observe my commandments and do them" (Lv 26:13), God will shower blessings on His people, will assure them of peace and prosperity, and will set up His dwelling among them: "I will be your God, and you shall be my people" (Lv 26:12).

But, on the other hand, if the people should turn away from the Torah, "if you will not hearken to me, and will not do all these commandments, if you spurn my statutes, and if your soul abhors my ordinances, so that you will not do all my commandments, but break my covenant, I will do (the same) to you" (Lv 26:14 ff.). God will turn away from His people, will break them, inflict terrible punishments on them and reduce them to extreme wretchedness. Yet, if they will only recognize their sin, humble themselves before the Lord and return to Him with all their heart, He will take pity on them and will bend down to them in mercy.

These are the "two ways" of Deuteronomy (30:15-20), which God offers to His people: "See, I have set before you this day life and good, death and evil. . . . I have set before you life and death, blessing and curse." Always and on all levels, the ultimate standard is the divine teaching, the Torah of the Lord, which is not an abstraction but essential reality: "For this Torah which I command you this day is not too hard for you, nor is it far off. It is not in heaven. . . . Neither is it beyond the sea. . . . But the Word is very near you: it is in your mouth and in your heart, so that you can do it" (Dt 30:11-14).

As Deuteronomy says, the Torah "is your life" (32:47): "The Lord your God will circumcise your heart and the heart of your offspring, so that you will love the Lord your God with all your heart and with all your soul, *that you may live*" (30:6). "Therefore choose life, that you and your descendants may live, loving the Lord your God, obeying his voice, and cleaving to him; *for that means life to you*" (30:19 f.).

The salvation which God offers to His people is the life of conformity to His will which fidelity to the Torah ensures. Neither life nor salvation can exist outside the Torah. The

Torah is a divine thing; it contains perfect revelation and has an eternal value: "Nor is it with you only that I make this sworn covenant, but with him who is not here with us this day as well as with him who stands here with us this day before the Lord our God" (Dt 29:14). The Torah contains all that God prescribes for Israel "throughout their generations, as a perpetual alliance" (Ex 31:16). "And as for me," God says through the mouth of deutero-Isaiah, "this is my covenant with them . . . : my spirit which is upon you, and my words which I have put in your mouth, shall not depart out of your mouth, or out of the mouth of your children, or . . . of your children's children . . . from this time forth and for evermore" (Is 59:21). [Deutero-Isaiah is the modern name given to chapters 40-55 of the book of Isaiah to indicate another author and date.]

The Torah is the expression and incarnation of "the holy covenant" (Dn 11:28.30) established between God and His people forever. The people will become unfaithful to its promises, but God, for His part, will always remain *shomer ha-berith,* "the faithful God who keeps covenant and steadfast love with those who love him and keep his commandments, to a thousand generations" (Dt 7:9; Dn 9:4; Neh 1:5; 9:32; 2 Chr 6:14): "He is mindful of his covenant for ever, of the word that he commanded, for a thousand generations" (Ps 105:8): "He confirmed to Jacob . . . a statute, to Israel . . . an everlasting covenant" (Ps 105:10): "He is ever mindful of his covenant" (Ps 111:5).

This is the basic idea that gives the key to understanding all that rabbinical tradition says about the Torah. Numerous passages in Scripture are traditionally taken as referring to the central position of God's teaching: "For I give you good precepts: do not forsake my Torah!" (Prv 4:2): "(Wisdom) is a tree of life to those who lay hold on her; those who hold her fast are called happy" (Prv 3:18): "Her ways are ways of pleasantness, and all her paths are peace" (Prv 3:17).

B. The Study of the Torah

"Study of the Torah prevails over everything else" (*We-talmûd Torah ke-neged kûlam*).[1] However, knowledge of the Torah as a way of salvation is not infused by God. In order to reach sanctity and attain salvation, one must put the precepts of the Torah into practice. Now, to do this correctly, one must know these precepts; and this is possible only through constant study. This line of reasoning introduces us to the heart of Jewish life and explains the great value which Judaism has always attached to the study of the Torah and the absolute necessity of such study. But the only real study is that which leads to true fidelity to God's word: "The essential thing is not study in itself but the action that flows from it," as R. Shim'on b. Gamliel (ca. 140 A.D.) says.[2] In the same place,[3] we find the saying of the ancient Hillel (beginning of the Christian era): "A man without instruction (in the Torah) cannot be a pious man." Every religious attitude that is not based on the principles of the Torah is necessarily a deviation.

The necessity of studying the Torah above everything else is well stated in a celebrated passage from the Mishnah:

> These are the things (to which the Torah) has fixed no limits: the corners (of fields, which must be left for the poor: Lv 19:9; 23:22); the first fruits (Dt 26:1 ff.); the *rayon* (the sacrifice offered by a private individual outside the three "pilgrimage" feasts: Ex 23:15.17; Dt 16:16 f.); good works; and the study of the Torah.
>
> And these are the things whose fruits a man eats here in this world but whose source is left to him for the world to come: honoring his father and mother; good works; making peace between a man and his neighbor; and the study of the Torah. But the study of the Torah surpasses all the rest.[4]

Through the Torah, Israel was associated with the sanctity of God and was herself thus sanctified. Studying the Torah and applying it to life are works of sanctification and are, at the same time, salvation and the permanent accomplishment of the main task that God had confided to His people.

C. Life According to the Torah

"Ben Bag-Bag says: 'Turn the Torah over again and again (in every sense), because everything is contained in it.' "[5] The teachers of tradition hold that the study of the Torah is immensely valuable and of imperative necessity only because such study allows one to keep the commandments. The *Tanna debe Eliyahû* says that a good knowledge of the Torah "renders the body alert for (carrying out) the commandments."[6] The man who knows the will of God will not miss any opportunity for conforming to it. Knowledge of the Torah also urges a man to do *ma'assim tovim,* "good works." It fosters the correct attitude so that he will, in practice, follow the way that the Lord has marked out for him. "In study, a man assimilates the contents of the Torah and the Mishnah (the oral Torah) and thus learns the fear of God and good deeds," which are "the end of all things."[7] Since this study places a man on the good path, it preserves him from all sin and transgression, thanks to the intimate knowledge it assures to him: "If the words of the Torah are present in a man('s heart), he will also know that he must not commit any transgression or (do) any displeasing action."[8]

Thanks to the Torah, Israel learned *derekh ereṣ,* correct conduct. "Blessed be the All-Present, blessed may He be, who has given Israel the words of the Torah so that they may teach her *derekh ereṣ* and that thus their sins may not be multiplied in the world."[9]

Knowledge of the Torah makes a man diligent in carrying out the commandments, intent on acting correctly and attentive to what he is doing. Not only that, but it also protects him from all his evil inclinations. "Blessed is Israel!" exclaims the Midrash. "When (the Israelites) are occupied in (the way of) the Torah and acts of charity, they exercise control over their propensity to evil."[10] He who studies the Torah and the Mishnah escapes ten enslavements, namely, the bad use of the eyes, the ears, the hands, the feet, the mouth and the body.[11]

Moreover, study of the Torah purifies a man from the sins that he may have committed:

> "How fair are your tents, O Jacob, your encampments, O Israel! Like valleys that stretch afar, like gardens beside a river. . . ." (Nm 24:5 f.). How can the purifying effect of rivers (be compared) to that of houses of study? Just as men who have become unclean enter the river

> (to take a purifying bath) and come out purified, so, too, those who are full of sins and enter houses of study, emerge purified.[12]

The nature of the Torah as a concrete way of salvation demands that study and knowledge of its contents be the prelude to keeping the commandments. Study and practice are inseparable.

The Midrash emphasises this fundamental idea. First, it describes the instructed man "who has in his mind a hundred teachings of Scripture, a hundred teachings of the Mishnah and a hundred answers from the Talmud," and who can, therefore, be compared to Moses and Aaron. Then the Midrash contrasts such a man with one who has in his mind "a hundred ideas of stealing, a hundred ideas of incest and a hundred ideas of murder."[13] Once more, the accent here is on the knowledge of the Torah which prevents a man from having evil thoughts that end by leading him into sin.

Yet the study of the Torah and the carrying out of the commandments are not one and the same thing. In itself, study is infinitely more precious than keeping the commandments: "All the *miṣwoth* (precepts) that a man practices in this world can give only as much light as a candle, while the Torah lights up the whole world from one end to the other."[14] Study and practice come from the same source, but the Torah is nevertheless richer in quality than the commandments it contains. This common source must be sought less in the fact that the Torah embraces the "613 commandments" than in the sovereign efficacy of the Word of God, due to which the practice of the Word is contained implicitly in the study of the Word.

The number 613 was arrived at by a talmudic computation. In *Makkoth,* we read: "R. Simlaï (ca. 25 A.D.) says: '613 commandments were revealed to Moses: that is, 365 (prohibitions), according to (the number of) days in the solar (year), and 248 (positive precepts), according to the members of the human body.' "[15]

A moral interpretation of these numbers is also provided:

> R. Yûdan bar Simon (ca. 230 A.D.) says . . . : "613 commandments were given on Sinai, that is, 248 positive commandments and 365 prohibitions: 248 positive command-

> ments— . . . each member (of the body) says to a man: 'I beseech you, use me to carry out such and such a commandment!': 365 prohibitions— . . . each day says to a man: 'I beseech you, do not commit such and such a sin today!' "[16]

What we have just said about the relationship between the *miṣwoth* (precepts) and the Torah applies equally to the relationship between the *miṣwoth* and *derekh ereṣ,* correct moral conduct. The Torah forms man's character and also provides him with the principles of correct moral behavior. Hence, in certain respects, the study of the Torah may be confused with correct behavior, which is, as it were, the natural prolongation of that study. Yet, in itself, the study of the Torah is greater than upright conduct, for it is the basis thereof and the source from which it flows.

The same can perhaps be said about repentance. The study of the Torah prepares man's heart for repentance. The Midrash explains this is a context which insists on the permanent nature of the effort of study: "No one should say: 'I have studied Scripture and the Mishnah today. Therefore, it is not necessary for me to do so tomorrow.' "[17]

In another passage, study is also related to repentance:

> If you see a man who has been instructed (in the Torah) committing a sin during the day, do not become indignant about it for the next day. Perhaps he will have done penance for it during the night (while studying the oral Torah), for it is said: "The Torah of your mouth is better to me than thousands of gold and silver pieces" (Ps 119:72); "Hatred stirs up strife, but love covers all offences" (Prv 10:12). There is no love apart from the Torah.[18]

D. Praise of the Torah and Study

"He who has acquired the words of the Torah has acquired the life of the world to come."[19] In a very large number of passages in rabbinical tradition, the teachers praise the Torah and its study as the central element in Jewish life. The following are a few of the many doctors of the Law who wrote in this strain: Simon the Just;[20] R. Ele'azar b. Pedat (died ca. 279 A.D.);[21] R. Meïr;[22] R. Shim'on bar Yohaï (ca. 150 A.D.);[23] R. Ele'azar b. 'Azariah (ca. 100 A.D.);[24] Rabba bar R. Hanna (ca. 280 A.D.);[25] R. Nehoraï (ca. 150 A.D.);[26] R. Yoḥanan b. Zakkaï (died ca. 80 A.D.);[27] R. Yossé b. Halafta (ca. 150 A.D.).[28]

Chapter VII

Prayer and Piety

A. Prayer, Piety and the Torah

For Judaism, the life of prayer and piety was not something separate from the rule of the Torah but an organic part of it. This is evident because, from the very beginning, one of the central elements of worship in the synagogue was the reading of the Torah, its translation into a language which those present could understand (*Targum*), and the reading of passages from the prophetical books (*Haftaroth*) during the Sabbath and feastday services. Preaching was also very important in the synagogue and consisted of homilies on the main points of the passages read and their haggadic development. In this fashion, worship helped to make the Jew familiar with the contents of the Torah and reminded him of the imperative necessity of making it the supreme norm of his life. Thus, too, the community as well as the individual, since both are inseparable, were put into contact with God through the Torah. Furthermore, sacred Scripture inspired much of the actual wording of the prayers.

B. The Structure of Prayer

For a long time, prayer in Judaism dispensed with special wording, for its value lay in its spontaneity and in the fact that it came straight from the heart.

The Mishnah says: "(When) anyone . . . makes his prayer into something stereotyped, that is, when he uses ready-made formulas, his prayer is not a supplication."[1] And the *Pirkei Aboth* recalls the same principle: "When you pray, do not make your prayer something stereotyped, but be (careful) to make it (an appeal to the divine) mercy and a supplication before God."[2]

In addition, the whole domain of prayer was considered to form part of the oral Torah; hence there was an unwillingness to fix it by writing it down. "Those who consign prayers to writing," says rabbinical tradition, "are like those who burn the Torah."[3]

But this does not mean to say that public and private prayers dispensed with all types of structure. There were fixed times for prayer—at first, in the morning and afternoon, at the time of the two "perpetual" sacrifices in the Temple; and later, in the evening also, with a supplementary prayer (*mussaf*) on feast days. Moreover, the prayers themselves were well arranged. They were originally built around the recitation of the *Shema Yisraël* (Dt 6:4-9; 11:13-20; Nm 15:37-41) and the accompanying blessings.

Another important prayer was the *tefillah* (prayer *par excellence*), also called *amidah,* since it had to be recited standing, or "the Eighteen Blessings," after the number of praises contained originally in it. According as the liturgical heritage was enriched, and because of the absence of prayer rituals, the correct recital of prayers in public worship required increasing skill and had to be confided to men who had the requisite qualities.[4] Moreover, tradition demanded that the Scripture readings and the prayers be chanted, which called for musical ability, although at first it was only a question of recitative or, at most, of quite simple melodies.

C. The Synagogue Takes Over

Even while the Temple was standing and functioning, a fully developed synagogal system had existed side-by-side with it. And it was this system which, after the destruction of the Temple in 70 A.D., was able to substitute for the Temple and prevent the formation of a liturgical void. While the Temple stood, the Jews were careful to respect its character as a *miqdash* ["a holy place or sanctuary"], and hence as the only "sanctuary," in the strongest sense of the word. For this reason, they had always insisted that there should be differences between the performance of those ceremonies that were common to the Temple and the synagogue; for example, in the manner of giving the blessing of the Aaronites ["sons of Aaron": "priests"]. After the destruction of the Temple, certain usages proper to the sanctuary were introduced into the synagogue, *zekher la-miqdash,* "in memory of the Temple."[5] The teachers also insisted very strongly on the superiority of prayer over sacrifice: "Prayer is greater than sacrifice, because it is said: 'What to me is the multitude of your sacrifices?' (Is 1:11). And it is likewise said: 'When you spread forth your hands . . .' (Is 1:15).[6]

Around the same time, too, there was a tendency to make the synagogue a *miqdash me'at,* according to the passage from Ezekiel (11:16), which the Targum paraphrases as follows: "I have given them synagogues, which take second place after my sanctuary."[7] It was about this time, also, that the teachers took definite steps to safeguard the sanctity of the places of worship.[8]

Rabbinical tradition also insisted strongly on the especially meritorious nature of community prayer in the synagogue.

Whenever ten Israelites, the quorum necessary for public prayer, gather in the synagogue, the *shekhinah* [the presence of God] is among them.[9]

> Whoever frequents the synagogues and houses of study in this world, thereby acquires the merit of frequenting them in the world to come as well. . . . The Holy One, blessed may He be, says: "Who has ever come to my synagogue without finding my glory there?"[10] A man's prayer is nowhere heard (as surely) as in the synagogue, for it is said: "Have regard . . . to the cry and to the prayer which your servant . . . offers toward this place" (1 Kgs 8:28) . . . . The Holy One says: "Whoever prays with the community is regarded by me as if he had freed me and my children from the grip of the peoples of the world."[11] He who prays in the synagogue offers to God,

> so to say, a pure sacrifice, . . . as it is said: "Just as the Israelites bring their cereal offering in a clean vessel to the house of the Lord" (Is 66:20).[12] Every time the Israelites, in the synagogues and houses of study, cry out: "May His great name be blessed!", the Holy One . . . nods His head and says: "Happy the king who is praised in his own house!"[13]

The Jews continued to pray that the Temple would be rebuilt, and they were conscious that, in the hierarchy of religious values, the synagogue could never really be compared to the sanctuary. This is well expressed in a passage from the *Midrash Tehillim*:

> (The Lord) prefers the gates of Sion to every (other) dwelling of Jacob. . . . The Holy One . . . says: "I truly love the synagogues and houses of study, but which (place) do I love the most? It is Sion, because my (real) palace is there."[14]

D. Evolution of the Liturgy

Throughout the Talmudic period, prayer and the liturgy of the synagogue continued to develop and deepen, with the result that the teachers frequently had to make new regulations. At the same time, the prayer formulas tended to become stabilized. But this evolution did not always follow the same lines in Palestine as in Babylonia, an eventuality which is at the origin of the differences between the various prayer rites that developed in Judaism.

From about the seventh century on, the *piyyut*,[15] or synagogue poetry, began to emerge, and it influenced certain parts of traditional prayer, especially that which was used on the feast days.

The first liturgical poets whose names we know are Yannaï and Ele'azar ha-Qalir, and then, in the tenth century, Sa'adyah b. Joseph al-Fayyumi, head of the academy of Sûra in Babylonia. With Dunash ibn Labrat (tenth century), there began the golden age of the Spanish *piyyut*, the most celebrated representatives of which are Samuel ha-Naggid (993-1056 A.D.);

Solomon ibn Gabirol (from about 1022 to 1050), who was a philosopher among the poets; Judah ha-Levi (1075-1141); Moses ibn 'Ezra (beginning of the twelfth century); and Abraham ibn 'Ezra (middle of the twelfth century).

From Spain, the *piyyut* spread into Germany, where it excelled especially in the elegiac form (*seliḥoth* and *qinnoth*) with Moses and Meshullam b. Kalonymos (eleventh century), Yequthiel b. Moses of Spires, Kalonymos b. Judah (twelfth century), and Ele'azar b. Judah of Worms (thirteenth century). It also spread through all the countries in which Jews were living, and, in its turn, contributed to the differentiation between the prayer rites, of which the most widespread were the *minhag ashkenaz* (German rite) and the *minhag sefarad* (Spanish rite). The *piyyut* contained and conveyed mystical and esoteric elements as well as philosophical ones. Thus, in the course of the centuries, innumerable religious poets contributed to the enrichment of the liturgy of the synagogue.

The development of the liturgy and its increasing diversification in local usages made it necessary to compile prayer rituals.

The first collections of this kind go back to the Geonim (heads of schools) of Babylonia, such as Natronaï (eighth century) and 'Amram Gaon (ninth century), and consist mainly of directions for performing the liturgy correctly; for example, the texts of the prayers in 'Amram's ritual appear to have been added later. The first ritual properly-so-called that has come down to us is that of Sa'adyah Gaon (tenth century). Other famous teachers, such as Haï Gaon b. Sherira (939-1038), and the commentator on the Bible and the Talmud known as Rashi (R. Solomon b. Isaac of Troyes, 1040-1105), also composed prayer rituals. The most complete collection is the *Maḥzor Vitry* of R. Samuel of Vitry (about 1120), which also contains many religious poems.

From this period on, rituals and liturgical books were produced in abundance, mainly in the form of rituals for everyday use (*siddur*) or manuals for the feast days (*maḥzor*), a movement which gathered new impetus with the invention of printing. Leopold Zunz (1794-1886) listed no less than seventy-five different rites throughout the Jewish world, but there were really many more than that, although the differences were often minimal and purely regional.

E. The Language of Prayer

Rabbinical tradition insisted above all else on the necessity of making prayer an outpouring from the heart and laid down the principle that one could pray in any language.[16] Nevertheless, because of its essentially scriptural inspiration, prayer, and especially public prayer, was normally said in Hebrew. It seems, however, that Greek was very often the language of prayer among the Hellenistic Diaspora. The Jerusalem Talmud relates that, in the third century A.D., the *Shema* was still being recited in Greek in the synagogue at Caesarea. This led to a dispute among the teachers, who concluded that the essential thing was to pray in a language that could be understood. But with the deterioration of the political situation in Palestine, a certain amount of strain appeared in regard to the general use of Greek, which also happened to be the administrative language of the Asian province.

Opinions were divided about the liturgical use of Aramaic, the language commonly used by the Jews of Palestine and Babylonia. R. Judah ha-Nassi believed that it was better to use Aramaic for private intercessory prayer, while R. Yoḥanan b. Nappaḥa opposed this idea on the plea that the angels who were charged with bringing prayer before the throne of God did not understand Aramaic.[17] Yet some prayers in Aramaic were admitted into the ritual, the best-known being the *Qaddish,* the great prayer blessing the name of God. But by far the greater part of official and liturgical prayer was said in Hebrew, and when some reformers in the nineteenth century abandoned the ancient language, the traditionalists unanimously opposed the move.

F. The Value of Prayer

Jewish tradition considers prayer to be the highest expression of piety.

In a discussion between teachers as to whether or not prayer was a duty imposed by the Torah, R. Moses b. Naḥman (1195-1270: also called "Naḥmanides") opposed Maimonides and declared that prayer definitely ought to be considered an obligation, since one of the effects of God's grace is precisely that

He grants our requests when we invoke Him.[18] Because of his very nature, man should never cease praying, to affirm his complete depedence on God for everything. Since the essential element in prayer is *berakhah,* praise of God, R. Meïr (middle of the second century) required that every man should recite at least one hundred blessings each day.[19] The teachers were divided on the question of the length of prayer. As a general rule, they denigrated "the prayer of lip-service" and preferred a brief but fervent prayer. They felt that, in this area, one should proceed with the greatest caution and derive inspiration from the example of Moses, who composed a prayer of only five words when he was praying for his sister Miriam to be cured (Nm 12:13), but who spent forty days and nights in prayer on Mount Sinai.[20]

Prayer is always addressed to God, to the exclusion of every intermediary: "Man should not address himself to Michael or Gabriel, but to me," says the Lord, "and I shall hear and answer him without delay."[21] While it is legitimate to pray for our own needs, we are recommended to think first of others and their necessities. Those who pray for their neighbor will be heard first by God who will provide for their own needs at the same time.[22] Thus Moses prayed that sinners might repent, and he was heard.[23]

Prayer is always efficacious when it is said under the required conditions and inspired by an unalterable confidence in God.

When the prophet Isaiah told King Hezekiah that he was going to die (Is 38:1), the king replied: "Son of Amos, finish your prophecy and be gone! For I have a tradition from my ancestor David which says that, even if a man has the edge of a sword touching his neck, he should nevertheless continue to pray that he will be spared."[24] R. Ḥanina b. Dosa (ca. 70 A.D.) was renowned for the cures he worked by his prayers. He was even able to predict the result of his intercession because he could judge its effect beforehand by the facility with which he prayed.[25] R. Yoḥanan b. Sakkaï, head of the academy at Jabneh, had more confidence in R. Ḥanina's prayers than in his own. He said to his wife: "Although I am greater than R. Ḥanina where study is concerned, he is more effective in prayer. It is true that I am the prince, but he is the steward who always has access to the king."[26] Some teachers were of the opinion that prayer could even change something God had already decreed,[27] a point of view which some of the Hassidic teachers would adopt later on.

After the destruction of the Temple, the place of prayer above all others (see 1 Kgs 8:20), "an iron grille was placed between the Israelites and their Father in heaven," and "the gate of heaven was closed to prayer."[28] However, the pious man who prayed fervently and with an upright, pure intention, could always overcome that obstacle. To emphasize the link between prayer and the Temple as the place where the glory of God was present in an especially efficacious way, tradition taught that one should turn towards the sanctuary when praying. Still, anyone who did not know in which direction to pray, had simply to turn his heart towards his Father in heaven."[29]

The principal attitude of mind to be adopted in prayer was one of humble acknowledgement of the life that God gives man and of thanksgiving for all the good He pours out on him. In order to pray, one put oneself into the presence of God. When R. Yoḥanan b. Sakkaï lay dying, he said to his disciples: "When you pray, realize whose Presence you are in."[30]

The basic element in prayer was the intention. In Scripture, the prophet Amos exhorted the people to prepare themselves to meet their God (Am 4:12). From the verb used in this context, *kawwen,* was formed the term *kawwanah,* which expressed this fundamental frame of mind. Maimonides defined the word in the sense that man should free himself from every other thought and should place himself in the *shekhinah,* the presence of God.[31] It was especially the Jewish mystics of all schools who insisted on the necessity of a pure, upright *kawwanah,* of which perhaps the best definition is that given by Babyah ibn Paqudah in his *Duties of the Heart*: "Our aim in prayer ought to be nothing else than to stir up the soul to consume itself in the presence of God, raising itself up to its Creator, offering Him both praise and thanksgiving, and casting on Him everything that weighs it down."[32]

Chapter VIII

Trends in Spirituality

A. The Esoteric Trend

As one would expect, the mainstream of Jewish spirituality flowed through the official schools; and it was especially strong in those schools with Pharisee leanings. Yet, from ancient times, there were in Judaism other currents of spirituality which developed along with the schools, but which were conditioned by many external influences, cultural as well as political, and which were, moreover, part of the general evolution of ideas that occurred in the post-exilic period.

One of the major elements in the preaching of the prophets had been a "spiritual" reaction to an over-formalistic attitude to the prescriptions of the Torah; and as the ancient eschatological concepts changed with the deterioration of the political situation, this reaction showed itself more particularly in an apocalyptic form. Ancient biblical eschatology had been closely linked to historical evolution, but the new current partially transposed it into the expectation of a superterrestrial world. The same current, but in a different form, also ran through and nourished the various sects, just as it appeared, expressed in other categories of thought, in the spiritualizing interpretations of the Hellenistic Jewish authors (e.g. Philo of Alexandria, died 54 A.D.).

In official doctrine, the community always came first, and the individual was seen only as part of that community. But one of the special characteristics of the spiritual currents was the emphasis they gave instead to the personal, individual attitude, the piety and the conduct of the man who took up his position on the fringes of the official trends. This individualism was especially evident in the apocalyptic movement, which appeared as an *initiatory* knowledge, in contrast to the *talmud Torah,* the study of the Torah, which the official schools held to be an imperative duty for everyone without exception.

The same spiritual tendency appeared also in the sects, on the group level. Groups of men, inspired by the same ideals and sharing the same views on the "perverse" nature of society, deliberately chose to draw apart from the world, obeying a "rule" which would allow them to live on a spiritual level that seemed impossible to attain without this separation from corrupt society. The Maccabees had struggled heroically against the general cultural and spiritual levelling which the *diadochi* of Syria had sought to achieve in order to consolidate their rule over a territory inhabited by peoples of extremely different cultures. [The *diadochi* (Greek for "successors") were the Macedonian generals who fought over the empire of Alexander the Great after his death in 323 B.C.] But the Hasmonean dynasty, descendants of the Maccabees, had not lived up to the hopes raised by their forebears, and, consequently, the political situation had deteriorated even further. Accordingly, the tendency to withdraw from a wicked world was heightened, becoming a kind of "emigration inwards" that was to remain one of the characteristic traits of all the similar trends that were to appear in the subsequent course of Jewish history. This whole atmosphere was to give rise to the mystical and esoteric current which was closely connected, on all levels, with the "pietistic" movements.

The official schools showed a marked reserve in regard to these trends towards withdrawal from the world, an attitude which is explained by the fact that one of the basics of the official doctrine was precisely the deep conviction of Israel's profound solidarity *as a collective unit* in relationship to the Torah. At all levels, rabbinical tradition, following the teachings of the Bible, insisted that the revelation on Sinai was addressed equally to all Israelites: "Then Moses brought *the people* out of the camp to meet God; and they took their stand at the foot of the mountain" (Ex 19:17); "Then he took the book of the covenant, and read it in the hearing of *the people;* and *they* said, 'All that the Lord has spoken we will do, and we will be obedient'" (Ex 24:7); "Nor is it with you only that I make this sworn covenant, but with him who is not here with us this day" (Dt 29:14 f.). In such a point of view, there was obviously no room for a doctrine of initiation that could detract from the solidarity of the Jewish people by dividing it into initiates and non-initiates. Furthermore, the teachers of tradition considered that the eschatology preached in apocalyptic circles was too far removed from the biblical concept.

This reaction also explains why, in the end, only one apocalyptic work was admitted into the canon of Scripture, namely, the Book of Daniel, and why, in the whole of rabbinical tradition, no book of this type is quoted, again apart from Daniel. Yet apocalyptic ideas are to be found in rabbinical tradition, where they are prominent in the messianic concepts.

This mystical influence is discernible especially in the *Ḥagigah* treatises (Mishnah, Tosephta and the two Talmuds) of rabbinical tradition. For example, we learn that there was lively mystical speculation, mixed with gnostic ideas, but that, at the same time, the possible dangers to health and sanity were also stressed.

> Four (teachers) entered the *pardes* (the "orchard," from the Greek, *parádeisos*). In our context, the word means those metaphysical speculations by which one is, as it were, transported into the world above. Tradition interprets this term as being an abbreviation composed of the initials of the four senses of Scripture: 1) *peshat,* the literal sense; 2) *remez,* allusion; 3) *derash,* allegory; 4) *sod,* the mystical sense. (The four teachers were) Ben 'Azaï (R. Sime'on b. 'Azaï, Ben Zoma (R. Sime'on b. Zoma), Aḥer (R. Elishah b. Abuyah) and R. 'Aqiba. . . . Ben 'Azaï plunged deeply into this speculation and died (as a result). . . . Ben Zoma did the same and suffered a (grave) injury (for, by doing so, he lost his reason). . . . Aḥer cut down young shoots (by becoming a heretic). . . . Only 'Aqiba ascended in peace and descended in peace.[1]

From the same source, we know that the preferred objects of this type of speculation were the *ma'asseh bereshith,* the work of creation, and *ma'asseh merkavah,* the vision of the divine chariot in the Book of Ezekiel (1:4-28); and that it was forbidden to teach these things in public.[2] Here it was apparently a question especially of gnostic speculations; and the teachers' misgivings in this area were expressed in the following laconic way:

> If anyone gives himself up to speculations concerning the four things here mentioned, it would have been better for him if he had not been born: that which is on high (in heaven), that which is below (in the depths), that which existed before (the creation of the world), and that which will happen after (the end of the world).[3]

B. The Blending of the Esoteric Current with Tradition

Nevertheless, the traditional teachers' distrust did not prevent the esoteric currents from developing, as is evident from the large number of mystically inspired treatises that were written, the most ancient of which date from the fourth and fifth centuries, at the end of the Talmudic epoch.

These treatises are called collectively "the literature of the Hekhaloth" because they are almost always concerned with speculations about the "heavenly palaces" (*hekhaloth*), and therefore about the structure of the divine world. Those mainly responsible for transmitting this literature were several "tannaites" (teachers during the period 20-200 A.D.) who were regarded as "initiates," such as R. 'Aqiba b. Joseph, R. Eli'ezer b. Hyrkanos, and especially R. Sime'on b. Yohaï. About the same period, we find in Babylonia a group of mystics, the *Yordé merkavah,* whose speculations were concerned above all with the divine chariot, as their name implies. They contributed to the development of this literature, and their influence was also felt in the liturgy.

The *Sefer Yeṣirah* ("Book of Creation") is a mystical work that reflects the development of the esoteric current between the third and sixth centuries. It propounds a cosmogony and a cosmology that were influenced by gnostic and neo-Pythagorean ideas.

Gradually, the mystical and esoteric currents became part of Jewish tradition, along with the written Torah and the oral Torah, codified in the treatises of rabbinical tradition. It was true that the mystical trend had been molded by innumerable influences in the course of centuries, and that it had digressed and developed in its own special way. Yet it was nothing less than another approach to the Torah, for, when the *peshat* (literal sense) and the *derash* (allegorical sense) were superseded, the mystical tradition tried to fathom the deepest and most "interior" sense of the Torah. For this reason, it was called *hokhmah penimith,* "interior knowledge." Its ultimate aim was to show that the Torah was not only the supreme rule of life for the Jewish people but that it had a cosmic role to play, since it contained the plan of all creation. Thus he to whom the full meaning of the Torah was revealed became, by that very fact, a ruling power in the cosmos. This is an extremely important concept here, for it sums up the entire piety of mystical inspiration.

C. The Influence of Religious Philosophy

From ancient times, Jewish mysticism was deeply influenced by philosophical ideas, especially neo-Platonic and neo-Pythagorean ideas. This influence very naturally increased with the blossoming of religious philosophy in Judaism, which coincided with the beginnings of the Islamic period.

Very quickly, great centers of Jewish settlement in Palestine, North Africa and Babylonia fell under Moslem domination. Fruitful cultural exchanges were then established between the two communities, and after a short time, the Jews adopted Arabic as their literary and vernacular language. Islam believed in strict monotheism and had been largely inspired by biblical and rabbinical tradition. Hence, from a religious point of view, it was undoubtedly closer to Judaism than was Christianity, which had evolved in a pagan-Christian atmosphere. Moreover, by borrowing from Arab savants, Jewish intellectuals came into, or renewed, contact with the philosophy of antiquity. And under the influence of Moslem theology (*kalam*), Jewish thought left the exclusive domain of the Torah and opened up to philosophical thought.

The first religious philosopher of Judaism was Sa'adyah b. Joseph al-Fayyumi (882-942), head of the academy at Sûra in Babylonia. In answer to some disputed points in traditional teaching and its decisions in the Babylonian schools, and in order to refute the doctrine of the Karaïtes, who denied the legitimacy of the oral Torah and rabbinical tradition, Sa'adyah wrote his treatise *Emunoth we-de'oth* ("Faith and Knowledge," the title of the Hebrew translation, the original having been written in Arabic), a defense of the Jewish religion based on philosophical reasoning.

Jewish neo-Platonism first developed at Qairuan in North Africa, in what is now known as Tunisia, where there was an important Jewish intellectual center, and reached its peak in Spain with Solomon ibn Gabirol (about 1020-1070), who was later known to the scholastics as "Avicebron" or "Avencebrol," and whose principal work, *The Fountain of Life,* has been preserved only in Latin. His *Keter malkhuth,* "The Royal Crown," is very important for his ideas on creation and the birth of the world; it also found a place in Jewish liturgy, as an addition to the prayer for the eve of Kippur. In this context, we must also mention Baḥyah ibn Paqudah (eleventh century), who was more dependent on Islamic mysticism and whose *Duties of the Heart* nourished Jewish piety for many generations.

The Aristotelian trend was represented by Abraham ibn Daud (second half of the twelfth century); by Judah ha-Levi (1075-1141), author of *Sefer ha-Kuzari;* and especially by Maimonides (Moses b. Maïmon, 1135-1204), to whom we owe the *Guide for the Perplexed* (*Moreh nebukhim,* a Hebrew translation of the original Arabic), in which he tried to show the perfect compatibility between the data of revelation and those of reason.

D. German Hassidism

The movement commonly called "German Hassidism" was the first real pietistic trend in Judaism which started as a result of the influence of mystical and esoteric teaching.

We left the esoteric current with the *Yordé merkavah* in Babylonia (see above, Section B, in this chapter). In the eighth century, this current penetrated Italy, Spain and France, especially Provence. The Kalonymos family, which originated in Lucca, Italy, was responsible for spreading the mystical trend in Germany, where it appeared about 1150 with R. Samuel b. Kalonymos "the Pious." The most representative personages in this movement were R. Samuel's son, R. Judah he-Ḥassid ("the Pious") of Ratisbon (died 1217), and his disciple, R. Ele'azar b. Judah of Worms (died 1238).

Our knowledge of this movement comes mainly from the major document which it bequeathed to us, the *Sefer Ḥassidim,* the principal parts of which date back to R. Judah he-Ḥassid. The religious outlook of the German Hassidism was profoundly affected in its development by the cruel experiences of the First Crusade (1096). In German Hassidism, mysticism was for the first time united with a penitential discipline, one which, in this instance, was based on rules drawn up by R. Ele'azar of Worms.

The *Sefer Ḥassidim* contained rules of life intended for the pious Jew, to whom it pointed out his duties and obligations. In it, ethical teaching was "popularized" with the aid of many stories and anecdotes, etc. It greatly influenced the piety of German Judaism until the *Musar* ("ethic") of R. Isaac Luria took its place.

While not neglecting the importance of the Torah, R. Judah he-Ḥassid gave ethics absolute priority in the concrete circumstances of daily life and insisted on purity of intention, deep faith and permanent communion with God in prayer. In his introduction to the *Sefer Ḥassidim,* he says that he wrote the book exclusively for those who fear God and meditate on the nature of His Being. Thus knowledge of God surpasses everything else and can be attained through the *kavod* ("glory"; *dóxa* in Greek) of God, which has been revealed to us. On this point, R. Judah is indebted to the teaching of Sa'adyah Gaon, although German Hassidism links this *kavod* with elements borrowed from ancient mysticism.

Chapter IX
The Kabbalah

A. Development

The Kabbalistic system was the outcome of the encounter of Jewish mysticism and esoteric teaching with philosophy. In ancient rabbinical literature, the word *qabbalah* simply meant "tradition" and was the preferred term for the books of the Bible outside the Torah. Gradually, however, *qabbalah* became a synonym for *esoteric* tradition.

The state of this tradition before it was influenced by medieval philosophy can be gauged from the *Sefer Bahir,* the "Book of Light," a treatise composed without much care in Provence in the twelfth century, after the fashion of a Midrash, and based on borrowings from various older sources. In it, the mainly gnostic inspiration of ancient Jewish mysticism is clearly prevalent. The contents of the book are very varied; and the mystical interpretation of the Hebrew alphabet figures largely there.

Philosophy did not exert a direct influence on what was to become the Kabbalah. The adepts of the Kabbalah studied the philosophers, including the Arabic, Moslem ones, picked out the mystical elements in them and used these elements in their own discipline and in their own special way.

Among the writers of philosophy who thus had a lasting impact on the development of the Kabbalah, we must mention particularly Sa'adyah Gaon, for his doctrine of the *kavod*;

Baḥyah ibn Paqudah, for his ethical teaching with its central theme, *devequt,* union with God; Judah ha-Levi and Abraham ibn 'Ezra, for their speculations on the names of God; Solomon ibn Gabirol, for his theory of the will and the Logos; Abraham bar Ḥiyya and the neo-Platonic exegetes, for their theory of emanations, the structure of the soul and psychological elements; and, finally, Maimonides, for his theory of the active intellect as a cosmic force acting on those who had been "enlightened."

The first groups of Kabbalists appeared in Provence between the mid-twelfth and mid-thirteenth centuries. Their most prominent representative was R. Isaac the Blind (end of the twelfth to the beginning of the thirteenth century), son of R. Abraham b. David of Posquières, one of the principal adversaries of the philosophical teachings of Maimonides. R. Isaac bears the honorific title of "Father of the Kabbalah," and he was a classical example of the mystical contemplative. The Kabbalistic groups of Provence originated a whole pseudepigraphical literature, consisting of a large number of relatively slim volumes which were falsely attributed to teachers who had lived in ancient times. R. Isaac elaborated the terminology of the *Sefiroth,* which were ten metaphysical powers arranged in an ascending hierarchy and within which, the Kabbalists claimed, God's Being manifested itself.

R. Isaac kept in constant touch with the north of Spain, where, in the first half of the thirteenth century, there was a very active Kabbalistic center at Gerona, with teachers as famous as R. Jacob b. Sheshet and R. Moses b. Naḥman ("Nahmanides"). The anonymous treatise, *Temunah,* which inspired a rich literature of speculation on the divine names, was probably written at Gerona, too.

Under the influence of German mysticism, there was a revival of the ecstatic trend, of which the most prominent representative was R. Abraham b. Samuel Abulafia, who had received "enlightenment" in 1271 in Barcelona. In an impressive number of treatises, Abulafia developed his doctrine and technique of contemplation, the object of which was to remove the shell in which the human soul was imprisoned so that the soul could reach prophetic enlightenment. Abulafia led an adventurous life, getting himself involved, for example, in a messianaic movement and presenting himself in Rome, where he invited the Pope, Nicholas II, to embrace Judaism.

As a reaction against the growing influence which neo-Platonic ideas were then exercising on the Kabbalah, there was an appreciable return to the ancient ideas derived from gnosticism. R. Moses b. Sime'on of Burgos (end of the thirteenth century) was the most important figure in this trend, which was remarkable especially for its doctrine of an empire of diabolical emanations, the negative side, as it were, of the luminous world of the *Sefiroth.*

B. The "Discovery" of the Zohar

Towards the end of the thirteenth century, an event occurred that was to be of the greatest importance for the later development of the spiritualistic and pietistic currents in Judaism. A Spanish Kabbalist, R. Moses b. Shemtov of Leon (1250-1305), claimed to have "discovered" a mystical treatise in the form of a Midrash on the Pentateuch, the author of which was probably R. Sime'on b. Yoḥaï. According to the Talmud, R. Sime'on was reputed to have remained hidden in a cave for thirteen years, accompanied by his son, R. Ele'azar, in order to escape the persecution unleashed by the Romans in 135 A.D.[1] The treatise was the *Sefer ha-Zohar,* the "Book of the Splendor," and its attribution to R. Sime'on was entirely in keeping with the spirit of the Kabbalistic pseudepigraphs of the period. Actually, the *Zohar* had been written with the help of several more ancient elements, but generations of Kabbalists believed that it was an authentic, inspired work of R. Sime'on b. Yoḥaï.

Until the appearance of the *Sefer ha-Zohar,* the Kabbalistic trend had been expressed in a multitude of treatises of very diverse tendencies. But in the *Zohar,* the Kabbalah acquired a major document which, from then on, was recognized as the purest, most authentic and most authoritative statement of the esoteric doctrine. For this reason, it became the real Bible of the Kabbalists, to whose eyes it revealed the *razé Torah,* the secrets, and hence the true meaning, of the Torah.

The *Zohar* united and summed up the essential elements of the ancient mystical and esoteric tradition, such as its teachings about *adam qadmon* (primitive man), the *Sefiroth,* the *Mark-*

avah, the *Hekhaloth,* the mystical significance of letters and numbers, and the esoteric interpretations of the names of God.

C. The Kabbalah after the Discovery of the Zohar

The influence of the *Zohar* on the Kabbalists was felt from the moment the book appeared. One of R. Abraham Abulafia's disciples, R. Joseph b. Abraham Guiqatilia (1248 to about 1305), in his treatise, *Sha'aré orah* ("The Gates of Light"), gave a beautiful introduction to the mystical symbolism of the *Zohar.* Because of his competence and acknowledged authority in Talmudic studies, he helped to avert a split between traditional studies and mystical speculation. Since then, there have always been Talmudic scholars who have included the *Zohar,* and hence the esoteric tradtition, in their research, but without thereby becoming devotees of Kabbalistic teaching. This phenomenon is called the "rabbinical Kabbalah."

A special place among the adepts of the Kabbalah belongs to R. Isaac ibn Latif (end of the thirteenth century), who elaborated a system of mystical theology almost exclusively based on philosophical concepts. His principal work, *Sha'aré shamayim* ("The Gates of Heaven"), was intended to be the speculative counterpart of Maimonides' *Guide for the Perplexed.*

The evolution of the Spanish Kabbalah during the fourteenth century was connected principally with the school of R. Solomon b. Abraham b. Adreth of Barcelona (1235-1310), of which the most outstanding representatives were R. Baḥyah b. Asher of Zaragoza, and R. Shemtov ibn Gaon, who was the first Kabbalist to settle in Safed in Galilee (about 1325). The fourteenth century in Spain also produced two pseudepigraphical treatises, the *Sefer ha-Peliah* ("Book of the Prodigy") and the *Sefer ha-Qanah* ("Book of Acquisition"), Kabbalistic anthologies that had wide circulation throughout the Jewish world. Among others, these two treatises were devoted to an original criticism of the *Halakhah* ("juridical decision"), trying to prove that the Torah did not have an obvious sense and a mystical one, as traditional teaching claimed, but only a mystical sense which was the real, obvious sense. Ideas such as those propounded in these two treatises prepared the way for the complete ascendancy of Kabbalistic doctrine over the whole Jewish world.

The deterioration of the Jews' situation in Spain following the success of the Christian reconquest of the provinces from Moslem domination brought about a kind of "emigration inwards" and hence a reinforcement of the ecstatic, even apocalyptic, Kabbalah. Yet, while the speculations of the Kabbalists of this type were often extreme, they were confined to a relatively narrow circle of initiates.

As a result of the expulsion of the Jews from Spain in 1492, a catastrophe which contemporary authors compared to a third destruction of the Temple, the mystical and esoteric trend became the preponderant factor in Judaism for several centuries. Many renowned Kabbalists who were forced into exile spread their doctrine in the countries in which they settled.

D. The "Cenacle of Safed" and "Holy Ari"

In the first half of the twelfth century, there was an extraordinary concentration of Kabbalists in Safed in Galilee. The choice of this town was not just a random selection. In nearby Meron lay the tomb of R. Sime'on b. Yoḥaï, who was considered the supreme master of esoteric teaching and author of the *Zohar*. Moreover, the district around Safed was hallowed by the tombs of many masters from the period of the Mishnah [1-200 A.D.] who had taken refuge in Galilee after the events of 135 A.D. and to whom the Kabbalistic tradition attributed various mystical traits. The Kabbalah gained the complete support even of such great Halakhists ["lawyers"] as R. Joseph Meraç and R. Joseph Qaro, author of the *Shulhan 'arukh,* the rabbinical compendium which, from the sixteenth century on, became a universal authority.

The upheaval caused by the expulsion from Spain gave a new impetus to messianic speculations, which were closely connected with the esoteric current. The teachers were largely of the opinion that the events which had led to their being driven from Spain, that choice land in which Judaism had known an unprecedented golden age, were nothing other than the *ḥevlé-ha-Mashiaḥ,* the portents of the messianic era.

While R. David ibn Zimra (died 1573) still represented the "classical" Kabbalah, the new current found its foremost theologian in R. Moses Cordovero (1522-1570), whose speculative system, set down in his two treatises, *Pardes Rimmonim* and *'Elima Rabbati,* departed notably from the ancient Kabbalah. An important number of teachers came under Cordovero's influence, among them being his own teacher and brother-in-law, R. Solomon Alqabeṣ, and his disciples, R. Abraham Galante, R. Eli'ezer Askari, author of the *Sefer Harēdim* ("Book of the Fearful"), R. Samuel Gallico, R. Mordekhaï Dato, and R. Abraham Azulaï.

At Safed, associations, which one could, in fact, call brotherhoods, were formed with the idea of putting the mystical teachings into practice in daily life. These fraternities played a decisive part in the formation of the pietistic current which spread rapidly from Safed to the rest of the Jewish world.

Yet in the "cenacle of Safed," there was one man whose name and teaching are closely associated with the victory which the Kabbalah was to gain in the Jewish world. This was R. Isaac b. Solomon Luria (1534-1572), called "holy 'Ari' (or 'Lion')" from the initials of his name and title, *ha-ashkēnazi R. Isaac* ("R. Isaac of German origin"), or *ha-elohi R. Isaac* ("the divine R. Isaac"). Luria was the only Kabbalist at Safed who was not of Spanish origin, since his parents had come from Germany or East Europe. He was much less a theologian than R. Moses Cordovero, his teacher; and his system was based almost entirely on contemplation and meditation. He added some original elements to the Kabbalah as it was presented in the *Zohar,* and placed almost exclusive emphasis on mystical contemplation, prayer and *tiqqun,* man's action in the great effort at restoring creation, which had been corrupted by sin. *Tiqqun* was to culminate in the arrival of the messianic era, which man could therefore "hasten" by the intensity of his piety and union with God. Luria expected the Messiah to come soon and, shortly before his death, revealed to his disciples that he himself was the Messiah, son of Joseph, who, according to the Talmud, was to be the precursor of the Messiah, son of David.

E. The Kabbalistic System of the Zohar, *and Luria's Contributions*

The essential difference between the Kabbalistic system and rabbinical teaching was the fact that the Kabbalah admitted a plurality of metaphysical powers considered as so many emanations from the Divine Being. These powers were principles of God's action, as they manifested themselves in the *Sefiroth,* or different modes of revelation, as expressed by the different names of God. According to the Kabbalah, this plurality of supernatural powers did not in any way affect the absolute unity of the Divine Being, who transcended the world while still being spiritually immanent to it. The first divine principle, which was the very basis of God's oneness, could never be attained by mystical speculation, for it was *en sof,* "the Infinite." For creation to have been possible, God had, as it were, to leave His isolation by a progressive unfolding of the potentialities inherent in His Being. The principle of creation was the "first existing being," called *adam qadmon* ("primitive man"), or *ze'er anpin* ("the one with the short face"), who proceeded, by a condensation of being, from the first divine principle as it unfolded and which was therefore called *arakh anpin* ("the one with the long face"). This principle of creation, *adam qadmon,* unfolded in its turn through different degrees of density until, finally, the world of physical creation was reached. The Kabbalah admitted four "worlds of creation," which were so many creative powers: *'olam ha-aṣiluth,* the world of emanation; *'olam ha-beriyyah,* the world of creation; *'olam ha-yeṣirah,* the world of formation; and *'olam ha-assiyah,* the world of action. The Kabbalah incorporated ancient ideas into its system and regarded these four worlds as the final blossoming of a process of evolution, in the course of which many analogous worlds, designed by *malkê Edom,* "the kings of Edom," appeared but only to disappear again.

In its progressive unfolding, the divine principle appeared as diversified in the ten *Sefiroth,* which, according to some authors, together formed the *adam qadmon* ["creative principle"], or the *kavod* ("the glory of God"), and was identical with the contents of the highest world of creation, that of the *aṣiluth.* The spiritual currents that circulated within the *Sefiroth* came together at the center of the Sefirotic system, which is the sixth *Sefirah,* called *Tifereth* ("Magnificence"). These currents then descended, with the *ze'er anpin* ("the one with the short face"), represented by another Sefirotic combination, to the tenth and final *Sefirah, Malkhuth* ("Royalty"). From this *Sefirah,* which was in direct contact with the material world, the Sefirotic system exercised a permanent beneficial influence on the whole of creation. The most important of the numerous Sefirotic combinations was a sort of supreme trinity (he who knows, he who is known, and knowledge), which was prolonged in seven other *Sefiroth* bearing the element of first knowledge concentrated in this trinity. The "Sefirotic tree," with its right-hand, middle and left-hand columns, was a very well-known image.

The *Zohar* also liked to represent the vital relationships that existed between the different *Sefiroth* and the Sefirotic combinations by comparing them to the relationships between the sexes. Thus everything seemed finally to be ruled by the relationships between a primitive male principle (*abba,* "father," or *melekh,* "king") and a female principle (*imma,* "mother"; *matrona,* "matron"; or *shekhinah,* "glory").

There was another polarization within the Sefirotic system, so that the "right-hand column" appeared as the concentration of the positive forces, while the "left-hand column" joined together the negative forces, which thus formed the *sitra aḥara,* the "other side," the world of demons.

At this level, Luria's system made an original contribution. In his view, the possibility of a creation beginning from the inaccessible *en sof* ("the Infinite"), and hence the possibility of the establishment of communications between two spheres as intrinsically different as the world of God and that of creation, was explained with the help of the doctrine of the *ṣimṣum,* the self-limitation of God, which was made possible by the introduction of a first negation within the very Being of God. In this way, a first line of demarcation was drawn, thanks to which the creation of things external to God became possible. Already in the ancient Kabbalah there existed a kind of polarization of forces and influences towards the very interior of the Sefirotic system. Thus, to return to the image of the Sefirotic tree, the "right-hand column" embodied the positive influxes, while the "left-hand column" was the expression of the *sitra aḥara,* the world of evil. According to Luria's conception, the *sitra aḥara* appeared after an initial cosmic drama called "the breaking of the receptacles," wherein, by a great increase in the inflow of divine light (*shef'a*), the light-receptacles of the *Sefiroth* were broken. The fragments of the receptacles then fell into matter, where they formed the *kelippoth* ("rinds"), the impure world. The work of *tiqqun* ("restoring") consisted principally in freeing the sparks of light which had thus fallen into the world of the *kelippoth*.

In his structure, man reflected that of the *adam qadmon* and was found at the center of this world and of the polarization of the divine and other influxes, which were at work there. For the Kabbalists taught that, while evil had no real existence, its influence nevertheless made itself felt. The first man was an absolutely pure being who had dominion over the created world. The souls of all men to the end of time were contained in his soul. Thus in him the fundamental unity of the human race was perfectly attained. But after sin intervened, the luminous nature of man was darkened and he was subjected to a series of catastrophes, the Flood, for example. The correction of this situation began with the patriarchs and Moses, who were personifications of the Sefirotic forces. It was continued by revelation, by worship (to which the Kabbalah attributed very great importance), and by God's covenant with Israel as a prototype and privileged representative of humanity. And all this was done with a view to the final remedying of man's situation by the coming of the messianic era. The people of Israel were unique in the world (see 2 Sam 7:23) because of their selection as the prototype of humanity; and in them the metaphysical principles of the four "upper worlds" came together and united on the level of the material world of creation. In this way, the most characteristic trait of Israel's existence was its unity, which was, as it were, the reflection of the very unity of God in this world of ours. This function of Israel as an exemplar is a major feature of Luria's Kabbalah. Israel's roots were deep in the Torah, whose 613 commandments reflected as many rays of divine light into the soul of every Jew.

There was another central principle in the Kabbalah which could be called *the* central principle [of contemporary Judaism] because of the almost universal domination of the Kabbalah doctrine. This was the principle of the absolute correspondence of the worlds on high with the worlds below. Not only was man guided by superior forces that came from heavenly worlds, but he could exercise an influence that was sometimes decisive on those upper worlds. In this subtle exchange of influences, the initiative belonged to man. By his love of God, the purity of his intention (*kawwanah*), the fervor of his prayer and the intensity of his desire for union with God (*deveqûth*), he had, as it were, to clear a channel for the luminous influxes so that they could pour down from the upper worlds upon the created world. This central position of man was an image of the Messiah's place in the whole work of salvation.

Another point in the Kabbalistic system was the doctrine of *gilgul,* that is, metempsychosis [or the transmigration of souls], based on the neo-Platonic concept of the three levels of the soul. The angelic world, too, with its complex hierarchy, had an important part to play in this system, which, like the ancient Kabbalah, also developed the mystical meanings of letters and numbers.

F. Ari's Musar *and the Victory of His Kabbalah*

Ari's teaching and his development of the ancient Kabbalistic system influenced daily life through the *Musar ha-Ari,* that is, his ethical and ascetical doctrine and the mystical path which he had traced out and which would be a determining factor in all the pietistic trends in Judaism from then on.

Ari died in his prime as the result of an epidemic, and, like so many other spiritual teachers, left behind him almost nothing in writing. We owe our knowledge of his teaching to his disciples, and chiefly to his favorite pupil, R. Hayyim Vital Calabrese (1533-1620), who, in his treatise, *Eṣ ḥayyim* ("Tree of Life"), bequeathed to us the Kabbalistic system of his teacher.

For Ari's followers, only the writings of R. Hayyim Vital authentically conveyed their master's thoughts. However, it was impossible to prevent the spread of many other treatises which claimed him as their author but which were, for the most part, simply pious disquisitions on his teaching. Treatises of this type ensured the propagation of Ari's doctrine throughout the Jewish world, the most important ones being *Tiqqunê ha-teshuvah* ("Order of Penance"), by R. Abraham Zahalon; *Sefer ha-kawwanoth* ("Book of Intentions") by an anonymous author; and the *Shulḥan 'arukh shel ha-Ari,* a mystical explanation of the prescriptions of the *Shulḥan 'arukh* of R. Joseph Qaro, also by an anonymous author.

The Kabbalah not only instructed men about the process of creation but also strove essentially to show them the path of the reverse movement, the return of the soul to God. This return could be effected by a life of fidelity to the commandments of the Torah understood in their true, that is, their mystical sense. The goal of this path and the objective to be attained was *deveqûth,* union with God. There was much discussion as to whether the emphasis in this path should be on the love or the fear of God. Yet, wherever the emphasis was placed, *deveqûth* always left an unbridgeable abyss between man and God.

Ari also preached another way to union with God, that of mystical concentration and meditation, which freed the spiritual forces in the soul, thus allowing it to attain a real elevation. In this system, ecstatic rapture had a certain place, although it was not an indispensable element in it. Through mystical meditation, the soul gradually freed itself from all sense impressions and was made ready for "enlightenment." This meditation had to be done with a precise objective, which guided it on its perilous journey and which obtained for it spiritual impressions to replace those of the senses. This precise objective was the name of God in its many implications.

Prayer was another element of this mystical way, and, in prayer, the *kawwanah,* or becoming conscious of the mystical purposes that ought to guide and inspire the soul in its journey. In this concept, prayer appeared as an endeavor on man's part, leading him to travel through the realms of the spirit, and to follow the internal order of those realms while trying to bring about *tiqqun,* the restoration of that order wherever it had been disturbed by the negative influences coming from the *sitra aḥara,* the world of evil. In the *Sefer ha-kawwanoth,* Luria set up a comparison between man's actions and prayer. Man's actions, whether good or bad, influenced the external side of the worlds; and prayer, which was exercised interiorly, affected the real internal harmony between things in their immediate dependence on God, to the exclusion of every influence coming from the created world. As traditionally formulated, liturgical prayer reproduced the internal, hidden unfolding of the world process. The order of the spiritual world in its connection with time, which was manifested in the liturgy, shone through in the names of God contained in the prayers. The mystical action of the man who prayed consisted in the "liberation" of the divine name. The *kawwanah* thus became man's consciousness of the spiritual region through which he travelled in his prayer. The precise details of these matters are given in a rich literature derived from the *Sefer ha-kawwanoth* of Luria's school.

For Luria, the *kawwanah* went hand-in-hand with asceticism. He preached the imperative necessity of renouncing every pleasure afforded by the things of the world, but only insofar, of course, as such pleasure went beyond that which was indispensable for life. Nevertheless, every pleasure, even the necessary ones, given by a material thing, had to be purified and sanctified by the scrupulous observance of the religious rites and so "elevated" to a higher sphere. If a man was to be capable of spiritual elevation, he had to be permanently aware of his diminished state. The essential characteristic of Ari's *Musar* was its insistence on the necessity of a permanent state of contrition and penance for anyone who wished to raise himself up to the higher spheres and escape the domination of matter. Every possible means was to be used to favor whatever could help man to reach this essential frame of mind. As far as in him lay, man had to flee every dissipation and anything that might turn him from this path. In itself, such a search occupied a higher place in the hierarchy of values than the sole study of the Torah. Nevertheless, such study remained necessary, but here, too, it was the intention that counted most. Man had to study the Torah and keep the commandments fervently and enthusiastically. Furthermore, he had to practice the precepts for their own sake, because of their intrinsic worth, which their mystical sense revealed, and without any idea of reward.

The most expressive symbol of the interior purity that was essential in all these acts was the purifying bath that had to be repeated frequently and especially before morning prayer. Every action, even the most trivial, such as dressing, eating, or walking, had to be done as a mystical action, symbolic of the service of God.

Ari's *Musar,* popularized by his disciples, very soon extended its domination over almost the whole Jewish world and raised a veritable wave of mysticism. As one would expect, the purity of intention preached by the master was often distorted, so that, along with a real upsurge of piety, there was a spate of superstitious practices claiming his authority.

The most active promoters of the movement inspired by Ari were two of his disciples, R. Hayyim Vital Calabrese, as we have seen, and Israel Saruq. The latter won over a rich Italian rabbi, R. Menaḥem 'Azaryah of Fano, who went on to found a whole school of Kabbalists in Italy. Then Luria's Kabbalah spread to Germany, Bohemia, Poland and the countries of the East. The ways and customs that developed in the wake of this current, as well as some superstitious practices, were codified about 1600 by Moses b. Maḥir in his treatise, *Seder ha-yom* ("Order of the Day"), which inspired countless other collections (*Hanhagoth* and *Tiqqunim*).

The two treatises which did most to popularize Ari's *Musar* were the *Shnê luḥoth ha-berith* ("The Two Tables of the Law"), by Yesha'yah Sheftel Horowitz (died 1630), which was read especially by the Ashkénazim, and the *Ḥemdat yamim* ("Delight of Days"), which was favored by the Sefaradim.

The mystical movement associated with Ari's name and disciples left a profound impression on Jewish liturgy. It began a creative period during which the traditional ritual was enriched by a great number of new elements. Because of the influence of Ari's teaching, new prayers were introduced into the liturgy, such as the service of *Qabbalath Shabbath* ("Welcoming the Sabbath") on Friday evening before the evening prayer; that of *Yom Kippur qaṭan* on the eve of the feast of the new moon; and the *Tiqqun Ḥasoth,* the prayer of repentance recited at midnight in memory of the destruction of the Temple. New hymns of Kabbalistic inspiration also appeared, and passages from the *Zohar* were inserted into the ritual. But above all, in the very heart of the ritual, there appeared many *kawwanoth* which, from then on, were to accompany every act of religion. Many of these elements are still to be found in the book of traditional prayers and are a witness to the enduring influence of the Kabbalah of Ari.

Chapter X

Spiritual Development After Ari

A. General Situation: Shabbataï Ṣevi

From the end of the sixteenth century onwards, Judaism was dominated by the Kabbalah, which favored pietistic tendencies, but which also caused new messianic movements to spring up. Ari and his disciples had lived in constant expectation of the imminent arrival of the promised Liberator. This hope had been heightened by the strongly messianic character of Ari's doctrine, and it quite naturally encouraged the calculations and speculations by which devout Jews tried to determine the exact moment at which the Messiah would "manifest" himself.

During such a time of seething expectations, something was bound to happen. And it did in 1648, a year for which some Kabbalists had predicted the coming of the Messiah. A young adept of Ari's Kabbalah, Shabbataï Ṣevi by name, had spent several years cut off from the world, engrossed in the study of the *Zohar* and the writings of Ari's disciples. In 1648, in the synagogue at Smyrna, his native city, Shabbataï publicly pronounced the sacred tetragram, just as the High Priest used to do in the Temple in Jerusalem during the service of expiation on Yom Kippur, the Day of Atonement. By this action, he clearly indicated that he believed he was the Messiah. [The sacred tetragram was the name of God, from the Greek word, *tetragrammaton,* meaning the "four consonants" of the Hebrew name of God, YHWH, so sacred that it was not ordinarily spoken.]

Anathematized for his audacity, Shabbataï Ṣevi left his native city and began to lead a wandering life. But the movement he had started made rapid progress, due to the favorable circumstances then existing and the skillful propaganda of his "prophet," Nathan of Gaza. The Thirty Years' War had ruined many of the Jewish communities in Central Europe, and the Cossacks had decimated those in the Ukraine, so that distress was widespread and the climate was very propitious for Shabbataï's claims. Many reputable teachers declared he was genuine, just as R. 'Aqiba had once greeted Bar-Kochba as the Messiah, and almost everywhere Jews got ready to follow the Messiah who would lead them to the Holy Land.

Because Shabbataï was being acclaimed by his followers as the *King* Messiah, the Turks thought that the whole movement was politically dangerous and threw him into prison. There they gave him two alternatives, beheading or conversion to Islam. He chose Islam and then tried to justify his choice by appealing to certain vague references in the Talmud. But his apostasy caused bitter disappointment in the Jewish world.

B. Polish Hassidism

The last of the spiritualistic movements based on the teachings of Ari and his disciples took place in Poland. During the Crusades, Poland had been a welcome refuge for Jews fleeing from Germany, but the situation of their communities there had worsened all through the seventeenth century. The Cossacks, under their hetman (commander), Chmielnicki, had wiped out many Jewish communities. The Polish state, traditionally a protector of the Jews, was falling apart. The Catholic clergy insisted on the application of the anti-Jewish measures laid down in the canon law of the period, and the economic life and intellectual life of the Jews were profoundly affected as a result. The atmosphere thus created favored the formation of Kabbalistic circles influenced by Ari's *Musar,* especially as some of these circles were already in existence in most parts of the country. The best known representative of this trend at the time it began in Poland was R. Shimshon of Ostropol, who was martyred during the great massacre by the Cossacks at Polnoy in 1648.

The agitation aroused by Shabbataï Ṣevi continued in Poland, where crypto-Shabbatarian sects persisted even after the "Messiah" of Smyrna had defected to Islam. The Frankist movement, an offshoot of one of these sects, was founded by Jacob Frank (about 1726-1791), who was later converted to Catholicism, as Shabbataï Ṣevi had embraced Islamism. Towards the end of the seventeenth century, Ḥayyim Malakh, a disciple of Shabbataï Ṣevi, and R. Jodah Ḥassid, a renowned Kabbalist from Sjedlce, founded a sect whose members led an austere life in conformity with Ari's *Musar,* while professing an ecstatic messianism, and who called themselves the *Ḥevrat Ḥassidim* ("Fellowship of the Pious"). Their relationship with the rabbinical authorities were very strained.

In Poland, the teaching of the Kabbalah also favored magical practices, and a number of *Ba'alé shem* ("Masters of the Divine Name") appeared who claimed to be able to work miracles because of their knowledge of the divine names. The *Maggidim* were popular preachers, often without fixed abode, who travelled around the country preaching in the synagogues; and it was they in particular who had familiarized the people with the doctrine of Ari, the teacher from Safed. Even such renowned Talmudic scholars as the celebrated R. Moses Isserles of Cracow (about 1525-1572), author of an authoritative commentary on the *Shulḥan 'arukh,* studied the Kabbalah fervently.

For a very long time, Poland had also been one of the great centers of Talmudic scholarship. But now, as the political and economic situation grew steadily worse, many hitherto flourishing houses of study were declining, and the number of those who were able to engage in long years of study diminished rapidly. A gap was opening between the scholars, who were proud of their knowledge and convinced of their superiority, and the great mass of the people, who hadn't had much education.

Such was the general situation at the time of the "manifestation" of R. Israel b. Eli'ezer (1700-1760), or *Ba'al shem tov,* usually abbreviated to "Besht," who was to take pity on the wretchedness of the people and bring them a message of liberation. Besht was of humble origin and lacked great Talmudic erudition, a deficiency which his adversaries did not fail to reproach him with. He spent the first years of his life in obscurity, and partly in solitude, in the forests of the Carpathians, where he was probably in contact with the crypto-Shabbatarians. In any case, Besht was a fervent practitioner of the *Zohar* and of Ari's *Musar*. At the beginning of his public career, he led a wandering life, but he settled down in Miedžybož, on the borders of Podolia and Wallachia, a region which became the center of the Hassidic movement.

While Besht's doctrine was essentially based on Ari's system, it departed from it on one important point which partly explains the speed with which Hassidism spread and took root, and which made it a movement of liberation. According to Besht, one should serve God in joy, sustained by the knowledge that the whole universe is filled with the glory of God. But preaching this joyous way of life, Besht freed his *Hassidim* from the gloomy narrowness fostered by Ari's *Musar,* which required its followers to be always sad and troubled, to avoid scrupulously all contact with the impure world, and to submit to complicated rites of purification. In Besht's view, there was only one way by which man could approach God, the way of fervor (*hithlahavuth*) and joyful service.

One did not have to be either an "initiate" or a scholar to follow this way. Instead, it was open to everyone, because God was concerned only with each man's heart and inmost intention (*kawwanah*). A humble, unlearned man who had an intense desire to be united with God was more agreeable to the Creator than the greatest of scholars whose heart was dried up and whose piety was cramped and formal. Men had no reason to be sad: they knew that they had a Father who loved them, who was all-merciful and who only wanted to welcome them. Everything in nature, even the humblest things, spoke to them of the presence of God, His infinite bounty and His loving kindness.

Thus Hassidism became the way of the man in the street, to whom it opened up spiritual horizons he had not even dared dream of before. Besht did not propound his doctrine in learned expositions, written in technical language, as did the Talmudic scholars of the time. Instead, he went out to meet the people in the markets, the fairs and the inns. He spoke to them in language they understood, and, as the Haggadists had so skillfully done in former days, he used parables to teach them. This was the Hassidic method of instruction, at least during the first years, and, because of it, the doctrine of the Kabbalah became truly popular.

Besht believed that the essential thing was the desire to serve God. But how was one to serve Him? The best way was by prayer. Ari had attached a mystical value to liturgical prayer, but Besht, while maintaining this principle, was not much concerned about special formulas and times for prayer, although he did adopt Ari's ritual and the Sephardic rite for his followers. He taught that it was better to pray fervently when the heart was moved than to observe the liturgical rules and times scrupulously. Real prayer removed a man from all preoccupations; he was transported into another world and began to live in a way that would have seemed miraculous to him before. Like Ari's Kabbalah, Besht preached disinterested prayer, centered on God and the divine world. Such a prayer had a creative power, and its effectiveness was in direct proportion to the degree of *deveqûth* (intensity) attained by him who prayed. By his prayer and all his actions, man had to bring about *tiqqun* ["restoration"] and free the divine sparks that had fallen into matter. Thus the whole of a man's life, especially his relationships with others, became a prayer and a service to God.

In his dealings with his neighbor, a man was to be inspired by he maxim of the *Pirqe Aboth*: "Judge everyone favorably."[1] Creation, the work of God, was good because its contents reflected the Creator's perfection. Man had been created in God's image, and what seemed to be bad in him was often only a degree of the Good which we could not see. On this point, Besht returned to the old Kabbalistic conception of the subjective non-existence of evil.

He who was inspired by this teaching and put it into practice in his life became a *Ṣaddiq,* a just and supremely perfect man, who, because of his high degree of perfection and elevation of soul, became for his brothers a guide in the way of Hassidism and an intermediary between God and man. He was like a bridge that linked the upper and lower worlds; he was like Jacob's ladder, with its foot resting on the earth, but with the *shekhinah,* the glory of God, shining at the top. For the *Ṣaddiq* to do this, he had to be close to his brothers, take their sufferings to heart and try to elevate them with him. And this demanded great humility.

C. Development of Hassidism

The established rabbinical authorities greeted some parts of Besht's teaching with reserve. First of all, the rabbis regarded Besht himself as an *'am ha-areṣ,* a peasant with no background in Talmudic scholarship, and hence they challenged his right to set himself up as a spiritual teacher, a duty which they considered was reserved to Talmudic experts. And did he not say that sincere piety was more important than the study of the Torah? And did he not thereby belittle the first duty and principal obligation of every Jew? Did he not encourage his followers to have little respect for established liturgical rules? Had he not adopted the Sephardic rite in a region where the Ashkenazi rite was compulsory? The rabbinical authorities advanced these and many other arguments against the *Ḥassidim,* thus feeding the fires of contention between Besht's followers and their avowed adversaries, the *Mitnagdim.*

From the beginning, everything about Besht was redolent of the miraculous, for his fervent admirers credited him with numerous miracles and extraordinary exploits. This attitude was characteristic of the Hassidic movement, but it prevents us from getting to know the real, historical man. Like Ari, Besht wrote little or nothing, and most of what circulated under his name was apocryphal. Everything we know about him was handed down to us by his disciples, especially by his "chronicler," R. Jacob Joseph of Polnoy, author of several treatises, the most widely distributed being *Toldot Ya'aqov Yossef* and *Ben Porath Yossef,* which give the broad outlines of Besht's teaching.

In R. Jacob Joseph, Besht had recruited a disciple who was a renowned Talmudic scholar, as he had done also in R. Dov Baer, the great *Maggid* ("preacher") of Mezritch, who was to succeed him as leader of the movement. Under R. Dov Baer, Hassidism continued to expand rapidly and to penetrate into White Russia and Lithuania, that bastion of rabbinism, where several renowned Talmudists, such as R. Israel of Polozk, R. Menahem Mendel of Vitebsk, and R. Shneür Zalman of Liosna, joined the movement.

The last-named began a particular Hassidic trend called the *Ḥabad,* an abbreviation from the initials of the words *ḥokmah* ("wisdom"), *binah* ("discernment"), and *da'at* ("knowledge"). The *Habad* was an attempt at uniting Hassidism with philosophy; and R. Schneür Zalman expounded his doctrine in his treatise *Tanya,* which appeared in 1796. Feeling that their stronghold was being threatened, the adversaries of the *Hassidim* grouped themselves around the greatest Talmudic authority of the time, the Goan ("eminent scholar") R. Eliahu of Vilna, and, in 1781, the great anathema was pronounced against the followers of the movement.

But this did not stop the rapid progress of Hassidism. After the death of R. Dov Baer, successor to Besht, the period of Saddiqism began, during which the Hassidic movement divided up into a very large number of "dynasties," each headed by a *Ṣaddiq,* a charismatic leader. However, because the office of *Ṣaddiq* came to be hereditary in most cases, this development held within it the germs of rapid decay for Hassidism.

The most renowned teachers after the death of R. Dov Baer, the great *Maggid,* were R. Elimelek of Lezajsk, R. Yeḥiel of Zloczow, R. Abraham Malakh (son of R. Dov Baer), R. Pinḥas of Kored, R. Naḥum of Czernobyl, R. Barukh of Tulzyn (Besht's grandson), and R. Levi Isaac of Berdyczew. Led by R. Menahem Mendel of Vitebsk, three hundred *Ḥassidim* settled in Palestine in 1778.

Rivalry soon sprang up between the various "dynasties" of the *Ṣaddiqim.* The best known "dynasty" was founded by R. Nahum of Czernobyl, whose son, R. Mordekai, had, in his turn, eight sons, who divided their father's "dynasty" among them. This "dynasty" was rivalled by that of R. Israel of Ružin, great-grandson of R. Dov Baer, who settled in Sadagora in Bukhovina, where he set up his sumptuous "court," which was frequented especially by the *Ḥassidim* of Austrian Galicia. The "dynasty," too, had many branches. In Poland, also, there were numerous Hassidic centers, each grouped around a local *Ṣaddiq.*

Besht's grandson, R. Naḥman of Brazlav, was a poet and

a particularly interesting figure. He rightly considered the fragmentation of the *Ṣaddiqim's* "dynasties" a danger to the spirit of the Hassidic movement. The most powerful and influential "dynasty" of the Polish *Ṣaddiqim* in the second half of the nineteenth century was that in Gora Kalvarja (Ger), near Warsaw, so much so that the rabbi of Ger was called "the emperor of the *Ḥassidim.*"

D. The Lifestyle of the Ḥassidim

Hassidism developed what was perhaps the most characteristic lifestyle of all the pietistic movements in Judaism. Despite their many differences, all the *Ḥassidim* followed Ari's ritual of prayers, a fact which distinguished them from the non-*Ḥassidim* around them; and, in addition, they had their own private oratories (*shtibl*) everywhere. The center of Hassidic life was the "court" of the *Ṣaddiq,* to which the individual *Ḥassid* went several times a year, according to his means and preferably on the occasion of the feasts, to consult the holy man and listen to his teaching.

The *Ṣaddiq* usually gave this teaching during the *agapés* [feasts of brotherly love] which were eaten on the Sabbath, and especially during the third Sabbath repast, in the afternoon (*se'udah shelishit,* or *shalshides*). The Ṣaddiq presided at table and distributed to his disciples leftovers from the dishes served him (*shirayim*). For the *Ḥassidim,* the *Ṣaddiq's* table was a real altar, and his function was comparable to that formerly carried out by the priest in the Temple at Jerusalem. During the Sabbath meals, canticle after canticle (*zemiroth*) was sung.

Music occupied an important place in Hassidism, for, through it, the *Ḥassid* took part in the *'olam ha-niggum,* "the (heavenly) world of melodies," and almost every *Ṣaddiq* had his personal *niggun.* Inspired by this music and by the *Ṣaddiq's* words, the *Ḥassidim* would begin dancing and would often go on and on almost interminably, especially on the *Simḥath Torah,* the feast of the Torah at the end of the feast of Tents. Often the *Ṣaddiq* himself took part in the dance, and then the *Ḥassidim* would say: "The *shekhinah* is dancing." Even after they had returned home, the *Hassidim* kept in contact with their *Ṣaddiq.* They would meet regularly in the oratory of their group to speak about the great feats of their holy man.

Even the death of the *Ṣaddiq* did not mean the end of the privileged bonds existing between him and his faithful followers. Through death, the *Ṣaddiq* entered the upper regions, where he was even more actively concerned about his people. Although in a different way, he continued to listen attentively to those who came confidently to his "holy tomb," leaving there their written requests, just as they had approached him while he was alive.

Although the *Ḥassidim* led a life apart, they did not cut themselves off entirely from the Jewish community. The anathema which had been launched against them at the beginning soon lapsed, and a working agreement satisfactory to all was reached. The *Ḥassidim*, did, of course, avoid any prolonged contact with the *Mitnagdim*, but their life was still ruled by the very same laws, those of the *Shulḥan 'arukh*. They respected the Talmud as the authentic expression of the oral Torah, although they reserved a special veneration for the *Zohar* and the innumerable treatises which, like the *Shibhe ha-Besht* ("Praises of Besht") and the *Keter shem tov* ("Crown of Good Fame"), related the great deeds of the founder of their movement and his disciples.

E. Modern Times

Hassidism was the last of the spiritualistic and pietistic movements in Judaism. We should perhaps also mention analogous phenomena in other countries affected by the teaching of Ari's Kabbalah, such as Morocco and Algeria. But these were usually cults dedicated to a particularly revered teacher which had many features in common with the Moslem veneration of an individual marabout.

The beginning and development of Hassidism in Eastern Europe coincided with the period of Moses Mendelssohn (1729-1786) in Germany and with the start of the era of "emancipation" which totally altered the nature of Judaism in the countries affected by it. On the contrary, however, most of Eastern Europe remained under Russian domination and so was unaffected by this change. As a result, the traditional structures survived there, for the most part, when they had been completely destroyed in Central and Western Europe.

Nevertheless, Hassidism was not to escape the fate of all "revivalist" movements. To a great extent, it was to become bogged down in routine, while Saddiqism would contribute greatly to its downfall. Hassidism reacted strongly against all the forces which, towards the middle of the nineteenth century, were overthrowing the traditional structures. Hence the enthusiasts for the emancipation and cultural assimilation of the Jews into the surrounding world regarded it as a bastion of orthodoxy and obscurantism, a verdict that was excessive and unjustly prejudiced. Despite all the manifest symptoms of decay, the Hassidic community continued to generate real spiritual power until it was wiped out between 1935 and 1945.

In the rest of Judaism, the struggle began between the "modernist" and traditionalist tendencies, with the latter losing as the result of a general, irreversible evolution. It is true that even the "reformers" tried to preserve a certain Jewish substratum, which, however, was often only a vague deism with a Jewish label. It was now that Judaism, within the short space of thirty or forty years, emerged culturally from the Middle Ages and mingled with the modern society of the nineteenth century. It was not a period favorable to spiritualistic movements. The most pressing concern was the need to preserve a Jewish identity despite a strong tendency towards assimilation, which in many cases resulted purely and simply in the abandonment of every Jewish tradition.

Nevertheless, in the midst of this whirling storm of ideas, there appeared in Russia a spiritualistic movement which tried to combat the progressive disintegration of the Jewish ancestral inheritance by a return to the real ethic of Judaism. This was the *Musar* movement, originated by a great Talmudist, R. Israel Lipkin Salanter (1810-1883). Somewhat as Besht had done, R. Israel saw the withering effect that purely intellectual Talmudic study could have on one's piety and moral attitude. Shortly after settling in Vilna, which was then the Talmudic capital of the world, R. Israel founded a society called *Hevrat Musar* for the study of treatises on religious morality. Under his influence, several treatises of this type were republished, among them being the *Tiqqun middoth ha-nefesh* ("Manual of the Qualities of the Soul") by R. Solomon ibn Gabirol, and the *Messilath Yesharim* ("The Way of Upright Men") by R.

Moses Ḥayyim Luzzatto (1707-1746), an Italian poet and Kabbalist. And it was not long before the society began to spread.

After settling in Kovno in 1848, R. Israel organized similar associations whose position within the Jewish community was analogous to that which Hassidism had occupied when it first began.

The fiercest opponents of the "Musarniks," as the followers of R. Israel were called, were R. Aryeh Leib Shapira, rabbi of Kovno; R. Yehoshu'a Heshel, rabbi at Yanova; and R. Yesha'yah of Salant. Despite this opposition from the rabbinical authorities, the movement made rapid progress. In 1872, R. Simḥah Sussel built at Kelm, in the district of Grodno, an oratory and house of studies dedicated to the study of ethical literature and a certain type of ecstatic piety. R. Simḥah later became director of the famed Yeshivah (Talmudic academy) at Slobodka. However, he did not have R. Israel Lipkin's spiritual resources, and the movement began to decline.

The direction of the *Musar* movement then passed to R. Isaac Blaser of Kovno, who, in 1879, went to St. Petersburg (modern Leningrad), where he tried to interest the young candidates at the official rabbinate in his doctrine. This action profoundly angered several influential rabbis, including the well-known R. Elḥanan Spector of Kovno. Later R. Blaser established at Lubtch, in the district of Minsk, a Yeshivah which had the support of many communities and which was intended for the education of rabbis imbued with the spirit of the *Musar*. R. Blaser left Kovno in 1902 and went to live in Palestine. The direction of the movement was then entrusted to R. Yeisel, who, although he had hitherto lived the life of a recluse, showed that he was a talented administrator. Other Yeshivoth became affiliated with the movement, the most important being the one at Slobodka, part of which was transferred to Hebron in 1923 and then to Jerusalem. The great Yeshivah of Mir, in Poland, was one of these affiliates, too.

The *Haskalah* ("Movement of Lights") in the countries of Eastern Europe and, as a general rule, the modern Jewish thinkers with rationalist tendencies, seldom had any real understanding of the spiritual values of the Hassidic movement and saw only the externals, with the result that they regarded its teachings as mere folklore, outdated and anachronistic. The *Ṣaddiqim* had taken up the cudgels for the ultra-traditionalist positions, thereby joining, in their own way, the ranks of Jewish orthodoxy while it was in the painful process of reconstruction after the devastation orthodoxy had suffered during emancipation. Nevertheless, within its own communities, Hassidism was still very vigorous. Martin Buber (1878-1965) made Hassidism known through his writings and helped to revive a real intellectual "neo-Hassidism" in various places. To him was due in great part the fact that Western Judaism, and indeed the whole Western world, came to appreciate the spiritual values and profound inspiration of Hassidism.

The progressive secularization of all aspects of Judaism and the influence of rationalism on Jewish thought had brought about great changes in Jewish life during the nineteenth century. In addition, there had been a general decline in Jewish studies and a progressive weakening of religious influence, properly so called. The cumulative effect of all this was that Judaism began trying to express its identity in areas other than the traditional ones. In countries affected by emancipation, the Jews at first seemed to wish to keep their identity only in the purely religious sphere. But the Dreyfus affair in France in 1894 proved a rude awakening because the Jews then saw that Western European society had rejected their desire to be integrated into it. Following this disillusionment, the Viennese author and journalist, Theodore Herzl (1860-1904) published his pamphlet, *The Jewish State,* which led in 1897 to the creation of the modern Zionist movement, whose aim was to give the Jewish people "norms" for the creation of a national state. But at this point another factor intervened to show how difficult, if not impossible, it was to try and divide Jewish life into independent segments.

Zionism had set out to be, in principle, a purely political movement, with no reference to Jewish religious tradition. But the Jewish masses of Eastern Europe, who were deeply rooted in the religious and spiritual traditions of Judaism, brought pressure to bear on the Zionists, who, as a result, had to preach the creation of a national homeland in Palestine, "the land of Israel," the Promised Land of the Bible and the object of pious hopes during the long centuries of exile. Thus the movement which was to achieve so much and have such a profound effect on contemporary Jewish life, had to graft itself on to the great Jewish and spiritualistic tradition. But despite this, at first almost all the leaders of orthodoxy, including those of the *Ḥassidim,* were resolutely hostile to Zionism, which had been launched and represented in great part by men who were detached from the religious traditions of Judaism and who were therefore considered as "impious."

The Jewish world in Central and Eastern Europe, and with it the ancient Hassidic world, were engulfed in the storm of the years from 1939 to 1945, which marked the end of an age-old history. This catastrophe, the worst that the world of Judaism had ever known, had a deeply traumatic effect on the Jewish consciousness. At one time, one might have expected that the reaction to such a shock would have been a revival of spiritualistic trends, but although such a revival did occur, it was very limited and found no expression within the Jewish religious establishment. The efforts of the Jewish consciousness to find and rebuild itself were mostly channelled into the creation of a Jewish state in Palestine in 1948. At present, this state has become the "reference point" of Jewish identity for most of the Jews throughout the world.

As regards the historical spiritualistic trends, we must mention the revival of several Hassidic movements in the United States, such as those represented by the rabbis of Lubavitch (*Ḥabad*: see above, Section C, *Development of Hassidism*), Szatmâr, Bobov and others. The Lubavitch movement is noteworthy for its openness. It has set up "Lubavitch centers" in many countries, maintains a whole network of schools and is very active in the "interior mission." In their anxiety to preserve their identity, these movements have kept the dress, language and customs of their former days in surroundings that are vastly different from those of their countries of origin. But despite their rather anachronistic character, they have attracted a certain number of young people who had been almost completely de-Judaized but who are now seeking for Jewish identity and authenticity. Thus, in some respects, these movements perform in Judaism the function which the Pentecostal fundamentalist trends perform in some sectors of Christianity.

The modern Jewish state has become a center of Jewish

consciousness and identity, but for those concerned about Jewish traditions, it will reach its true significance only when it evolves into a center of authentic Jewish values also. It could then become a new source of piety and spirituality, expressing itself in categories of thought different from those of the past but still drawing its inspiration from the old historical values. In this way, as many Jews now realize or suspect, the Jewish state could be an important step towards the realization of ancient "messianic" hopes and could contribute greatly to carrying out the still unchanged task of the Jewish people of leading the world to the knowledge of God and His revelation.

Appendix

SOURCES

by Roger Le Déaut, C.S.Sp.

Judaism is composed of many trends, some of which are expressed in the documents which have come down to us. In their choice of sources, writers who describe Judaism are often influenced by the ideas they have already formed of it, some of them relying mainly on the rabbinical data, while others stress the apocalyptic writings, which they regard as more significant. In fact, however, all the sources must be used to form a true picture of ancient Judaism in its rich diversity. It would be a mistake to build up an artificial synthesis, a kind of averaging-out, of the beliefs and practices of what is called normative Judaism. Certain movements, such as that of the sectarians of Qumran, do have specific traits. Yet the elements which are common to all the trends are more numerous and more important than any to be found in individual movements. These common elements are, above all, the essential data of biblical religion, which, however, we cannot pause to enumerate here. Suffice it to say that texts such as the Pentateuch [the first five books of the Bible], the prophets and the psalms are at once the source and the expression of Israel's piety.

Here, then, we present a survey of our main textual sources of information on the spirituality of Judaism, properly so called.

A. The Later Protocanonical and Deuterocanonical Books

["Canonical" roughly means "accepted" or "approved";

"proto-" means "first"; and "deutero-" means "second." The protocanonical ("first-accepted") books of the Old Testament are those which, from the beginning, were accepted by all as inspired. The deuterocanonical ("second-accepted") books are those whose inspiration was doubted or denied by some for a time; they are: Tobit, Judith, Wisdom, Sirach, Baruch, 1 and 2 Maccabees, the last six chapters of Esther, and three passages in Daniel—3:24-90; 13; 14. Catholics hold that both the protocanonical and the deuterocanonical books are inspired, and they distinguish them carefully from the apocryphal (non-inspired) books. Jews and Protestants, however, place the deuterocanonical books among the apocrypha; that is, they do not regard these books as inspired. The following shows the difference between Catholic terminology and that used by Protestants and Jews:

Catholic		Jewish and Protestant
Protocanonical books (inspired)	=	Canonical books (inspired)
Deuterocanonical books (inspired)	=	*The Apocrypha* (not inspired)
The Apocryhpa (not inspired)	=	*The Pseudepigrapha* (not inspired)

All Catholic Bibles contain both the protocanonical and the deuterocanonical books since the Church holds that they are inspired. Most modern Protestant editions of the Bible give the protocanonical books as the main body of the Old Testament and have the deuterocanonical books, which they call the *Apocrypha,* in an appendix.]

Our main sources of information on early Judaism are the books of Jeremiah and Ezekiel, in which we find the tendency towards "Judaism" already expressed, and also 1 and 2 Isaiah and the later prophets, with whom the rabbinical tradition claimed continuity. Then there is the Chronicler's synthesis (1 and 2 Chronicles, Ezra and Nehemiah), 1 and 2 Maccabees, Jonah, Job, Qoheleth (Ecclesiastes), Wisdom, Sirach, Tobit and Judith, which are typical of the religion and piety of Judaism before the Christian era.

B. The Apocrypha (Pseudepigrapha)

The *Apocrypha* present special problems, such as the question of dating, the scope of their influence, the degree to which they were accepted and the extent to which they underwent Christian retouching. Yet they are still the most fruitful and most used source of information on our subject.

The principal *Apocrypha* are:

Ethiopic Enoch (or *1 Enoch*), a large part of which may date from about 170 B.C. The second section (Chapters 37-41) is not verified by the Qumran documents. [These are documents which were discovered near the Wadi Qumran, at the northwest corner of the Dead Sea, in the late 1940's and early 1950's. They are also known as the "Dead Sea Scrolls." They consist of various scrolls and fragments of biblical and non-biblical writings which have added greatly to our knowledge of the history of the Old Testament text as well as of Jewish history and Hebrew literature in the period between the Old and New Testaments.]

The Book of Jubilees (about 150 B.C.), of which fragments in Hebrew were found at Qumran.

Th Testaments of the Twelve Patriarchs (about 150-100 B.C.).

The Psalms of Solomon (middle of the first century before Christ): these reflect the extent of the anti-Hasmonean spirit prevalent among pious Pharisees after Pompey's capture of Jerusalem in 63 B.C. [The Hasmoneans ruled Israel from 134 to 63 B.C. The Pharisees resented the secular spirit of the priest-king, John Hyrcanus I (134-104 B.C.); and Alexander Janneus (104-76 B.C.) put eight hundred Pharisees to death for their opposition to him.]

The Testament of Job, written in Greek, most likely in Egypt, during the first century A.D., and aptly described as "a pre-Christian document of missionary propaganda for Hellenistic Judaism."

The Assumption (or better, *The Testament*) *of Moses,* written between 7 A.D. and 30 A.D.

The Paralipomena of Jeremiah, written about 130 A.D.

The Book of Biblical Antiquities of pseudo-Philo, written before, and perhaps long before, 70 A.D.

4 Esdras, written towards the end of the first century of the Christian era.

The Syriac Apocalypse of Baruch, or *2 Baruch,* written at the end of the first century A.D.

The Apocalypse of Abraham, end of the first century of our era.

The Apocalypse of Moses, or *The Life of Adam and Eve,* before 70 A.D.

The Odes of Solomon come from a Judeo-Christian Gnostic background of the second century A.D.; the basic material is certainly Jewish.

C. Writings of Hellenistic Judaism

1. In the first place we must mention the Septuagint, a version of the Old Testament giving the sense in which ancient Judaism understood it and including in its text the religious concepts of the translators. Hence it is a precious testimony to the Jewish thought of the third century *B.C.*, and it had considerable influence on the religion of Greek-speaking Jews.

2. Philo of Alexandria (20 B.C. to 54 A.D.) wrote, among other things, a short treatise entitled *Contemplative Life* concerning the Therapeutae [who were apparently a branch or form of the Essenes, a name which probably means "The Pious Ones." The Essenes were a group of ascetics living in an isolated community under a rule, *The Manual of Discipline,* and somewhat like one of our stricter religious Orders. Most likely it is to them that we owe the Qumran documents or Dead Sea Scrolls.] Besides Philo, mention should be made of the work of Aristobulus (second century B.C.), from whom Eusebius quoted some fragments, and *4 Maccabees,* in which two other Alexandrian Jews gave their views on the observance of the Law.

3. Historians and apologists. Flavius Josephus (37-95 A.D.) is an important link between Palestinian Judaism and the Judaism of the Diaspora [of "the Dispersion," that is, those Jews who lived outside Palestine.] He is an invaluable source of information about the religious traditions of his era, especially the popular interpretation of Scripture.

Because of his works *Jewish Antiquities, The Jewish War* and

Life, we can rank him with other Jewish historians, such as Demetrius, Eupolemon and Artapan, of whom Eusebius has preserved some fragments recovered from Alexander Polyhistor (about 80-40 B.C.), or the author of *3 Maccabees* (end of the first century B.C.).

Important also is Josephus' *Against Apion,* which comes from a tradition of apologetic and propagandistic writings, as do the *Letter of Aristeus to Philocrates,* the now-missing *Sur Abraham* of pseudo-Hecateus, the fragments of pseudo-Phocylidus and pseudo-Menander; and especially the following work:

4. *The Sibylline Oracles,* the authentically Jewish parts of which (Books III, and IV-V, in part) date from about 140-130 B.C.

5. *The Slavonic Book of Enoch* (or, *2 Enoch*).

6. *Joseph and Aseneth,* an important work about whose nature and date there is much controversy.

D. The Writings Found in the Desert of Judah

These [Qumran] documents must be mentioned here because they help to throw light on the other trends in Judaism; and their numerous parallels with the New Testament prove that they are an independent source for a valid description of the Jewish religion of the first century of our era. But, while these discoveries provide good documentation on the Essenes of Qumran, we must be on our guard against extending to all the Judaism of that period the characteristics we find in the Qumran documents and making them our sole source of reference. The most significant texts for our purpose are *The Manual of Discipline, The Rule of the Congregation* and *The Damascus Covenant,* all of which deal with common life, prayer, asceticism, and the study of the Law. Then, too, there are the various biblical *Commentaries.*

E. The New Testament

Although Christianity was an innovation in Judaism, it was by no means a radical departure from it. Christianity first appeared as one Jewish movement among many others, and Christian theological themes, institutions and exegetical methods bear unmistakable marks of the background from which they emerged. But in using the New Testament, we must remember that it was composed in large part after the separation of Christianity from Judaism and that the picture it paints is not always unprejudiced and without bias.

F. Ancient Rabbinical Literature

1. The Targum, an Aramaic version of the Scriptures for use in the synagogue, shows how the Bible was interpreted, while its numerous paraphrases reflect the popular piety and common traditions of the time. [The Old Testament was written entirely in Hebrew, with the exception of two deuterocanonical books, Wisdom and 2 Maccabees, which were written in Greek, and a few short scattered passages in Aramaic. In the course of time, Aramaic replaced Hebrew in daily use, and Hebrew then became a dead language. Hence the ordinary Jew could not understand the Scriptures when they were read out in Hebrew in the synagogue. Accordingly, it became the practice to read some verses from the Hebrew Scriptures and then supply an oral verse-by-verse translation in Aramaic, called a *targum* ("translation," "interpretation").]

For a long time, the Targum was passed on orally, and only just before the Christian era was a beginning made to put it into writing, but not for use in public. At Qumran, several verses of Targums of Leviticus and Job were found in Cave 4 and a more complete Targum of Job in Cave 11. But a systematic compilation of the Targum was not really begun until the third century A.D. Thus two of the principal Targums, Onqelos on the Pentateuch and Jonathan ben Uzziel on the prophets, were based on the Palestinian traditions and appeared in their definitive form only about the fifth century A.D., in Babylon.

We possess two complete editions of the Palestinian Targum on the Pentateuch, the one known as that of pseudo-Jonathan and the one found in the Codex Neofiti 1 in the Vatican.

2. The Tannaitic *midrashim* contain the commentaries of rabbis before the third century A.D. [*"Midrash"* means "commentary"]:

The *Mekiltha* of R. Ishma'el on Exodus.

The *Mekiltha* of R. Simeon ben Jochai.

Siphra on Leviticus.

Siphre on Numbers and Deuteronomy.

Midrash Rabba, a commentary on the Pentateuch and on the *Megilloth* [that is, "the Five Rolls," namely, Song of Solomon, Ruth, Ecclesiastes, Esther and Lamentations].

The ancient *midrashim,* such as *Pesiqta Rabbati, Pesiqta Rab Kahana* and *Tanhuma.*

3. The Mishnah ("repetition"), compiled about 200 A.D., contains many ancient traditions about the feasts and worship of the second Temple.

The Mishnah and the Gemara ("completion"), that is, the first rabbinical commentaries on the Mishnah, formed the Talmud. The two great Talmuds were the Jerusalem, or Palestinian, and the Babylonian. [In both Talmuds, the Mishnah is substantially the same, but the Gemara in each is different since each Gemara came from a different school, Palestine or Babylonia.]

4. The traditions not collected in the Mishnah formed the Tosephta.

G. The Jewish Liturgy

The Jewish liturgy is the purest expression of traditional piety and contains elements that date from before the destruction of the Temple. Yet it must be subjected to critical study because some authors maintain that nothing in it was permanent before the Talmudic era.

Notes

NOTES TO CHAPTER 1

* Since this series is intended for English readers only, many references in the original article *Dictionnaire de Spiritualité* to publications in foreign languages have been omitted. All titles of primary sources have been translated into their English equivalents. When quotations from secondary sources are given in the body of the text, reference is made in the footnotes to the book or article from which the translation has been made.

[1] *4 Esdras* 14; Sanhedrin 21b.
[2] Horace, *Satires* 1.4.142.
[3] H. H. Rowley, *Worship in Ancient Israel* (London, 1967), pp. 213-245.
[4] S. B. Hoenig, *The Great Sanhedrin* (Philadelphia, 1953); H. Mantel, *Studies in the History of the Sanhedrin* (Cambridge, Mass., 1961).
[5] See J. Z. Lauterbach, *Rabbinic Essays* (Cincinnati, 1951), pp. 23-48.
[6] *2 Baruch* 85.3.
[7] *JA*, 13.5.9.; 18.1.2-6.
[8] *Aboth* 1.1.
[9] *JA*, 13.10.6.
[10] *Sotah* 22b.
[11] W. D. Davies, *Introduction to Pharisaism* (Philadelphia, 1967).
[12] *Aboth* 1.
[13] *Ten Years of Discovery in the Wilderness of Judaea* (London 1959), p. 92.
[14] See the *Damascus Covenant.*
[15] See *JW*, 2.8.4.
[16] *JW*, 4.3.9.

[17] *JW*, 2.81; *JA*, 18.1.6.

[18] See J. A. Montgomery, *The Samaritans* (Philadelphia, 1907); J. Macdonald, *The Theology of the Samaritans* (London, 1964), for the bibliography; J. D. Purvis, *The Samaritan Pentateuch and the Origin of the Samaritan Sect* (Cambridge, Mass., 1968), for a comprehensive view.

[19] G. F. Moore, *The Am ha-areṣ (The People of the Land) and the Haberîm (Associates)*, in F. J. F. Jackson and K. Lake, *The Beginnings of Christianity*, vol. 1, (London, 1920), pp. 439-445.

[20] M. Simon, *St. Stephen and the Hellenists in the Primitive Church* (London, 1958); W. D. Davies, *The Setting of the Sermon on the Mount* (Cambridge, 1964), p. 451; *Christian Origins and Judaism*, pp. 19-30.

[21] S. Lieberman, *Greek in Jewish Palestine* (New York, 1965); *Hellenism in Jewish Palestine* (New York, 1950).

[22] See W. D. Davies, *Paul and Rabbinic Judaism* (London, 1958), pp. 1-16.

[23] See J. Neusner, *A Life of Yohanan ben Zakkai* (Leiden, 1970).

[24] See G. F. Moore, *Judaism*, vol. 3 (Cambridge, Mass., 1930), pp. 17-23.

[25] See J. Goldin, *The Period of the Talmud*, in L. Finkelstein, *The Jews*, vol. 1, (New York, 1949), pp. 115-215.

[26] See J. Neusner, *A History of the Jews in Babylonia*, vol. 1, *The Parthian Period* (Leiden, 1965); vol. 2, *The Early Sasanian Period* (1966).

NOTES TO CHAPTER 2

[1] *L'essence du prophétisme* (Paris, 1955), p. 278.

[2] For the history of the development of concepts of covenant and a study of formularies of covenant, see D. J. McCarthy, *Treaty and Covenant*, coll. Analecta Biblica 21 (Rome, 1963).

[3] *1 Enoch* 89.

[4] *Jubilees* 10.1-9.

[5] Ibid., 15.31-32.

[6] Ibid., 16.18, 26.

[7] *4 Esdras* 5.23-29.

[8] *Biblical Antiquities* 12.8.

[9] *Assumption of Moses* 1.12; *4 Esdras* 6.55-59.

[10] *2 Baruch* 3.5-8.

[11] *Jubilees* 2.18-33.

[12] *Pirqe Aboth* 3.19.

[13] *JA* 18.3.1.55-59; *JW* 2.9.2.169-174.

[14] *JA* 18.8.2-9.261-309.

[15] *JW* 6.5.1.280; *Ta'anith* 29a.
[16] See *Pirqe Aboth* 1.3.
[17] Ibid., 2.20; G. F. Moore, *Judaism*, vol. 2 (Harvard, 1927), pp. 239 ff.; A. Marmorstein, *The Doctrine of Merits in Old Rabbinical Literature* (London, 1920; New York, 1968).
[18] 14.4-7.
[19] *On Sacrifices* 54.
[20] *JA* 18.5.2.117.
[21] *Manual of Discipline* 1-2.18.
[22] Ibid., 8.13-14.
[23] Ibid., 1.22-26.
[24] See *Hymns of Thanksgiving* 4.34.
[25] *Manual of Discipline* 3.3-9.
[26] Ibid., 4.19-22.
[27] *Hymns of Thanksgiving* 1.25-27.
[28] Ibid., 3.21.
[29] Ibid., 7.30.
[30] See *Manual of Discipline* 9.2-14.
[31] *Is God Unchangeable?* 107; *Allegory of the Jewish Law* 3; *Cain's Posterity* 42; *Who Is the Heir to Divine Things?* 103.
[32] *Who Is the Heir to Divine Things?* 98, 314.
[33] *Questions on Genesis* 3.60; *Allegory of the Jewish Law* 3.219.
[34] *Is God Unchangeable?* 134-135.
[35] *Questions on Genesis* 3.15.
[36] See B. J. Malina, *The Palestinian Manna Tradition,* (Leiden, 1968).
[37] R. Le Déaut, "Myriam, soeur de Moïse, et Marie, mère du Messie," *Biblica* 45 (1964) 212.
[38] *2 Baruch* 59.2.
[39] See *Ode* 12, on the Word.
[40] Philo, *Life of Moses* 2.51-51; see also *Letter of Aristeus* 143.
[41] See E. R. Goodenough, *By Light, Light: the Mystic Gospel of Hellenistic Judaism* (New Haven, 1935).
[42] *The Migration of Abraham* 39, 47; *The Confusion of Tongues* 92.97.146.147.
[43] See *Allegory of the Jewish Law* 3.177.
[44] *Cain's Posterity* 13-16.
[45] *Pirqe Rabbi Eliezer* 11, on the role of Adam.
[46] See *Manual of Discipline* 9.4-5.
[47] *Against Apion* 2.19.181.

NOTES TO CHAPTER 3

[1] J. R. Brown, *Temple and Sacrifice in Rabbinic Judaism* (Evanston, 1963).

[2] See R. De Vaux, *Ancient Israel: Its Life and Institutions* (London, 1961), pp. 321-330.

[3] *Commentary on Habakkuk* 12:7-9; *Damascus Covenant* 4.18; 6.11-14.

[4] B. Gärtner, *The Temple and the Community in Qumran and the New Testament* (Cambridge, 1965).

[5] See also the *Sibylline Oracles* 4.8-12, 27-30.

[6] M. Simon, *St. Stephen and the Hellenists in the Primitive Church* (London, 1958).

[7] *JW* 5.5.1-7; *Sukkah* 51b.

[8] *Life of Moses* 2.109-135.

[9] 96-99.

[10] E.g., *Tamid, Sukkah.*

[11] See A. Büchler, *Studies in Jewish History* (London, 1956), pp. 24-63.

[12] *JW* 8.8.7; see Philo, *On Flaccus* 46.

[13] *JW* 4.4.3.

[14] Ibid., 5.1.3; see also Philo, *Legation to Caius* 191.

[15] *JW* 7.8.7.

[16] See S. Safrai, *Pilgrimages at the Time of the Second Temple* (Tel Aviv, 1965).

[17] See Philo, *About Special Laws* 1.67-70; *Legation to Caius* 281 ff.; *JW* 2.19.1; Acts 2:9-11.

[18] *T. Gen.* 28:16; 49:27; 2 Mc 14:35—*skēnōseōs.*

[19] *M. Sukkah* 5.4.

[20] *T. Gen.* 28:17; *T.2 Chr.* 6:2; 33:13.

[21] Philo, *Life of Moses* 2.159.

[22] *JW* 5.1.3.

[23] Ibid., 6.2.1.

[24] Midrash *Lam. Rabba; Berakhoth* 32b; *M. Sotah* 9.15.

[25] Such as *4 Esdras* 9:44; 12:48; and *2 Baruch* 85:3; and the *Paralipomena of Jeremiah* 2:1-10.

[26] 4.8.

[27] *M. Ta'anith* 4.3.

[28] *M. Yoma* 7.1.

[29] See W. D. Davies, *Paul and Rabbinic Judaism*, pp. 256 ff.

[30] See A. Guttmann, "The End of Jewish Sacrificial Cult," *Hebrew Union College Annual* (Cincinnati) 38 (1967) 137-148.

[31] According to *Aboth* 1.2.

[32] See J. B. Segal, *The Hebrew Passover from Earliest Times to A.D. 70* (London, 1963).

[33] See Philo, *About Special Laws* 2.160.

[34] 17-18.

[35] *JA* 18.4.3.

[36] *M. Pesahim* 10.5.

[37] *Mekhilta Ex.* 12:42.

[38] See J. Migne, *Patrologia latina,* Paris, 26.184d.

[39] See G. Vermes, *Scripture and Tradition in Judaism* (Leiden, 1961), pp. 193-227; S. Spiegel, *The Last Trial* (New York, 1967).

[40] A. Neher, *Moïse et la vocation juive* (Paris, 1956), p. 127.

[41] 6.11; 14.20; 29.7.

[42] J. T. Milik, *Ten Years of Discovery in the Wilderness of Judaea* (London, 1959).

[43] *Manual of Discipline* 1, 2.

[44] Philo, *Contemplative Life* 65.

[45] *Shabbat* 88a; *Pesaḥim* 68b.

[46] *Aṣereth;* see *M. Hagigah* 2.4; *JA* 3.10.6. On a feast of mid-Pentecost, see J. Goudoever, *The Significance of the Counting of the Omer,* in *Studies in the Jewish Background of the New Testament* (Assen, 1969), pp. 64-86.

[47] *JA* 3.10.4; 13.13.5; compare *M. Sukkah* 4.9.

[48] *JA* 8.4.1.

[49] *M. Sukkah* 4 & 5.

[50] See R. E. Brown, *The Gospel According to St. John I-XII,* (New York, 1966), pp. 326-329.

[51] W. Harrelson, *The Celebration of the Feast of Booths According to Zach. XIV, 16-21, in Religions in Antiquity,* ed. J. Neusner (Leiden, 1968), pp. 88-96.

[52] 16.21-31.

[53] *JA* 12.7.7.

[54] *JW* 7.8.7.

[55] 50.8-12.

[56] *Damascus Covenant* 6.18; 10.14; 12.4.

[57] 50.12.

[58] *Biblical Antiquities* 11.8.

[59] J. Mann, *The Bible as Read and Preached in the Old Synagogue,* vol. 1 (New York, 1971), with an important introduction by B. Z. Wacholder.

[60] *Megillah* 75a.

[61] *Against Apion* 2.17.175.

[62] Ibid., 178.

[63] *Tos. Ta'anith* 2.5.

[64] Philo, *About Special Laws* 2.6.

[65] *Satires* 3.296.

[66] *Berakhoth* 8a.

[67] *Ta'anith* 2a. Concrete examples of this piety can be found in A. Büchler, *Types of Jewish-Palestinian Piety,* pp. 128-195.

[68] For Qumran, see *Manual of Discipline* 10.9 ff.

[69] *Berakhoth* 4.1-4.

[70] *JA* 4.8.13; *Tamid* 4.3; 5.1; and the phylacteries at Qumran.

[71] *Aboth* 2.13.

[72] *T. 2 Kgs* 2:12.

[73] *Sifre Nm* 12:13; *Berakhoth* 33b.

[74] See R. H. Charles, *The Apocrypha and Pseudepigrapha of the Old Testament in English*, vol. 1, p. 162.

[75] *Mekhilta Ex* 17:11.

[76] *T. Dt* 4:7; *Deut. Rabba* 3:24.

[77] See the *Damascus Covenant* 6.21; on the interpretation of Lv 19:18 in ancient Judaism, see D. Flusser, "A New Sensitivity in Judaism and the Christian Message," *Harvard Theological Review* 61 (1968): 107-127.

[78] See *T. Gen.* 35; *T. Deut.* 34:6.

[79] *T. Lv* 22:28.

[80] G. Vermes, *Scripture and Tradition in Judaism*, pp. 178-192.

[81] *T. Ex* 12:13; *T. Ez* 16:6; *T. Cant.* 2:9.

[82] H. Kosmala also sees a connection between the incident in Ex 4:24-26 and the salvation given to Israel through the blood of the Passover: see "The 'Bloody Husband,'" *Vetus Testamentum* 12 (1962) 14-28.

[83] 9.15.

[84] *2 Baruch* 9:2; 12:5; *Psalms of Solomon* 3:9.

[85] *Ruben* 1.10; *Judah* 15.4; *Simeon* 3.4, etc.

[86] 22.

[87] Tacitus, *History* 5.4: "Longam olim famem crebris adhuc jejuniis fatentur."

[88] I. Abrahams, *Studies in Pharisaism and the Gospels*, pp. 121-128.

[89] See also J. A. Montgomery, "Ascetic Strains in Early Judaism," *Journal of Biblical Literature* 51 (1932) 183-213.

[90] *Harvard Theological Review* 61 (1968) 97.

[91] J. T. Milik, *Ten Years of Discovery in the Wilderness of Judaea*, p. 54 f.

[92] E. F. Suttcliffe, *The Monks at Qumran as Depicted in the Dead Sea Scrolls* (London, 1960).

NOTES TO CHAPTER 4

[1] *Questions on Exodus* 2.36; see also *About the Virtues* 35; *About Special Laws* 3.155.

[2] 13:24.

[3] See D. Flusser, "A New Sensitivity in Judaism and the Christian Message," *Harvard Theological Review* 61 (1968) 107-127.

[4] *Sabbat* 31a.

[5] *About the Commandments* 51.

[6] *About the Virtues* 51; see also 95: *About Abraham* 208.

[7] *T. Dan* 5.3; *T. Issachar* 5.2; 7.6; *T. Benjamin* 3.3.

[8] 5.25 f.

[9] 6.20-7-2.

[10] 6.1.

[11] 9.3.

[12] Similar formulations are to be found in *T. Zabulon* 5.3 and in rabbinical literature.

[13] *T. Gad* 4.

[14] *Manual of Discipline* 1.8.

[15] Ibid., 5.20.

[16] Ibid., 11.7 f.

[17] *Hymns of Thanksgiving* 6.15 ff.

[18] *Damascus Covenant* 3.19; *Manual of Discipline* 8.8 f.; 9.6.

[19] See *Hymns of Thanksgiving* 6.25 ff.

[20] B. Gärtner, *The Temple and the Community at Qumran and the New Testament* (Cambridge, 1965).

[21] *About the Virtues* 175-186.

[22] *Pirqe Aboth* 3.18; *2 Enoch* 13.

[23] See H. A. Wolfson, *Philo*, vol. 2 (Cambridge, Mass.), p. 374.

[24] 187 ff.

[25] See in Eusebius: Eupolemus (*Preparation for the Gospel* 9.26), and Aristobulus (ibid., 13.12). Under the name Museus, Moses had been the teacher of Orpheus (Artapan: ibid., 9.27).

[26] Ibid., 9.29.

[27] *About Great Men* 54.

[28] *About the Confusion of Tongues* 95.

[29] *Life of Moses* 1.133-135.

[30] *About Special Laws* 1.97.

[31] *Questions on Exodus* 1.10, on the Pasch.

[32] *About Abraham* 98.

[33] *About Special Laws* 2.163.

[34] For the antiquity of this tradition, see G. Vermes, *Scripture and Tradition in Judaism* (Leiden, 1961), p. 210.

[35] See *Manual of Discipline* 8.7, 10; *Hymns of Thanksgiving* 6.18.

[36] 1.10.

[37] *About Rewards* 93-97; see also ibid., 163-165.

[38] See especially Philo, *On Flaccus*.

[39] Philo, *About Special Laws* 4.179 f.

[40] Philo, *Life of Moses* 1.65-70; see also *Ex. Rabba* 2.5.

NOTES TO CHAPTER 5

[1] Aboth 1.1.

[2] Pericope *be-ḥûqotaï* 8, p. 112c, ed. J. H. Weiss.

[3] *Qohelet R.* 1.13.
[4] *Tanḥ. Yitro* 11.
[5] 5a.
[6] *Megillah* 4.1.74d.
[7] See *Aboth* and *Aboth of R. Nathan*, at the beginning.
[8] *Tanḥ. Noaḥ* 3.
[9] *Nb R.* 14.4.
[10] 15.6.
[11] *Baba Meṣi'a* 33a.

NOTES TO CHAPTER 6

[1] *Péah* 1.1.
[2] *Pirqe Aboth* 1.17.
[3] Ibid., 2.5.
[4] *Péah* 1.1.
[5] *Aboth* 4.22.
[6] Page 139, ed. M. Friedmann (see bibliography below).
[7] Ibid., p. 87.
[8] Ibid., p. 111.
[9] Ibid., p. 79.
[10] Page 167.
[11] Ibid., supplement, p. 1 f.
[12] *Tanna debe Eliyahû*, ed. cit., p. 116 f.
[13] Ibid., p. 106.
[14] Ibid., p. 16 f.
[15] 23b.
[16] *Pesiqta of Rab Kahana*, ed. B. Mandelbaum (New York, 1962), 101a; and *Tanḥ. B.* pericope *ki téṣé* 2.
[17] *Tanna debe Eliyahû*, ed. cit., p. 195.
[18] Ibid., p. 16
[19] *Aboth* 2.7.
[20] Ibid., 1.1.
[21] *Pesaḥim* 65b; *Aboth* 7.7; *Sifra on Leviticus*, pericope *be-ḥûqotaï* 112, ed. Weiss (see bibliography below).
[22] *Sanhedrin* 59a.
[23] *Aboth* 3.4.
[24] *Ibid.*, 3.17.
[25] *Berakhoth* 35b.
[26] *Qiddûshin* 4.14.
[27] *Aboth* 2.8.
[28] Ibid., 2.12; 6.4; 4.9-10, etc.

NOTES TO CHAPTER 7

[1] *Berakhoth* 4.4.

[2] 2.13.
[3] *Tos. Shabbath* 14.5.
[4] *M. Ta'anith* 2.2.
[5] *Sukkah* 41a.
[6] *Berakhoth* 32b.
[7] See *Megillah* 29a.
[8] See *M. Megillah* 3.1-3; *Berakhoth* 26b-27a; *j. Megillah* 3.1.73d.
[9] *Mekhilta,* pericope *Yithro—ba-ḥodesh,* chap. 9, 73b, ed. Friedmann; see also *Pes. Rab Kahana* 193ab.
[10] *Dt R.* 7.1.
[11] *Berakhoth* 8a.
[12] *j. Berakhoth* 5.1.8d.
[13] *Berakhoth* 3a.
[14] On Ps 87:2; ed. Buber, p. 378.
[15] From the Aramaic *payyetan,* based on the Greek *poiétés.*
[16] *M. Sotah* 7.1.
[17] *Shabbath* 12b.
[18] *Sefer ha-miṣwoth,* tenth commandment.
[19] *Menahoth* 44b; *j. Berakhoth* 9.2.13b.
[20] *Sifré on Numbers* 105.28b, ed. Friedmann.
[21] *j. Berakhoth* 9.1.13a.
[22] *Baba Qamma* 92a.
[23] *Sotah* 14a.
[24] *Berakhoth* 10a.
[25] Ibid., 34b.
[26] Ibid.
[27] *Rosh ha-shanah* 18a.
[28] *Berakhoth* 32b.
[29] Ibid., 30a.
[30] Ibid., 28a.
[31] *Hilkhoth Tefillah* 4.16.
[32] 7.3.

NOTES TO CHAPTER 8

[1] *Ḥagigah* 14b ff.
[2] *M. Ḥagigah* 2.1.
[3] Ibid.

NOTE TO CHAPTER 9

[1] *Shabbath* 33a.

NOTE TO CHAPTER 10

[1] 1.6.

BIBLIOGRAPHY

Chapter 1

Ackroyd, P. E. *Israel under Babylon and Persia.* Oxford: 1970.

Albright, W. F. *From the Stone Age to Christianity.* Baltimore: 1946.

Bickerman, E. *From Ezra to the Last of the Maccabees.* New York: 1962.

Black, M. *The Development of Judaism in the Greek and Roman Periods (c. 196* B.C.-A.D. *135),* in *Peake's Commentary on the Bible.* London: 1962, pp. 693-698.

Brandon, S. G. F. *The Fall of Jerusalem and the Christian Church.* London: 1957; *Jesus and the Zealots.* Manchester: 1967.

Bright, J. *A History of Israel.* London: 1960.

Brown, R. E., Fitzmyer, J. A., and Murphy, R. E., eds. *The Jerome Biblical Commentary.* London: 1970.

Bruce, F. F. *New Testament History.* London: 1971.

Charles, R. H. *Religious Development between the Old and New Testament.* London: 1914.

Davies, W. D. *Introduction to Pharisaism.* Philadelphia: 1967; *Christian Origins and Judaism.* London: 1962; *Paul and Rabbinic Judaism.* London: 1958; The Jewish State in the Hellenistic World, in *Peake's Commentary on the Bible.* London, pp. 686-692; *Contemporary Jewish Religion,* ibid., pp. 705-711.

Driver, G. R. *The Judaean Scrolls.* Oxford: 1965.

Edersheim, A. *The Life and Times of Jesus the Messiah.* 2 vols. London: 1907.

Epstein, I. *Judaism.* London: 1959.

Farmer, W. R. *Maccabees, Zealots and Josephus.* New York: 1957.

Finkelstein, L. *The Pharisees,* New York: 1938; *The Jews.* New York: 1949.

Hoenig, S. B. *The Great Sanhedrin.* Philadelphia: 1953.

Lauterbach, J. Z. *Rabbinic Essays.* Cincinnati: 1951.

Leon, H. J. *The Jews of Ancient Rome,* Philadelphia: 1960.

Lieberman, S. *Greek in Jewish Palestine.* New York: 1965; *Hellenism in Jewish Palestine,* New York: 1950.

Macdonald, J. *The Theology of the Samaritans.* London: 1964.

Mantel, H. *Studies in the History of the Sanhedrin.* Cambridge, Mass.; 1961.

Montgomery, J. A. *The Samaritans.* Philadelphia: 1907.

Moore, G. F. *The Am ha-ares ("The People of the Land") and the Haberîm ("Associates"),* in Jackson, F. J. F., and Lake, K., *The Beginnings of Christianity.* Vol. 1. London: 1920, pp. 439-445; *Judaism.* Cambridge, Mass.; 3 vols. 1927-1930.

Neusner, J. *A Life of Yohanan ben Zakkai.* Leiden: 1970; *A History of the Jews in Babylonia.* Leiden: 1965-1966.

Pfeiffer, R. H. *History of New Testament Times.* New York: 1949.

Purvis, J. D. *The Samaritan Pentateuch and the Origin of the Samaritan Sect.* Cambridge, Mass.: 1968.

Ricciotti, G. *The History of Israel.* 2 vols. Milwaukee: 1955.

Rowley, H. H. *Worship in Ancient Israel.* London: 1967.

Russell, D. S. *Between the Testaments.* London: 1960; *The Jews from Alexander to Herod.* Oxford: 1967.

Sandmel, S. *The First Christian Century in Judaism and Christianity.* New York: 1969.

Scobie, C. H. H. *John the Baptist.* London: 1966.

Simon, M. *St. Stephen and the Hellenists in the Primitive Church.* London: 1958.

Tcherikover, V. *Hellenistic Civilization and the Jews.* Philadelphia: 1959.

Zeitlin, S. *The Rise and Fall of the Judaean State.* Philadelphia: 1962.

Chapter 2

Goodenough, E. R. *By Light, Light: the Mystic Gospel of Hellenistic Judaism.* New Haven: 1935.

Le Déaut, R. "Myriam, soeur de Moïse, et Marie, mère du Messie." *Biblica* 45 (1964) 212.

Malina, B. J. *The Palestinian Manna Tradition.* Leiden: 1968.

Marmorstein, A. *The Doctrine of Merits in Old Rabbinical Literature.* London: 1920; New York: 1968.

McCarthy, D. J. *Treaty and Covenant.* Coll. Analecta Biblica 21. Rome: 1963.

Moore, G. F. *Judaism.* Vol. 2. Harvard: 1927.

Chapter 3

Abrahams, I. *Studies in Pharisaism and the Gospels.* 2 vols. New York: 1967.

Brown, J. R. *Temple and Sacrifice in Rabbinic Judaism.* Evanston: 1963.

Brown, R. E. *The Gospel According to John I-XII.* New York: 1966.

Büchler, A. *Studies in Jewish History.* London: 1956; *Types of Jewish-Palestinian Piety from 70 B.C.E. to 70 C.E.* New York: 1968.

Charles, R. H. *The Apocrypha and Pseudepigrapha of the Old Testament in English.* 2 vols. Oxford: 1933.

Davies, W. D. *Paul and Rabbinic Judaism* . London: 1958.

De Vaux, R. *Ancient Israel: Its Life and Institutions.* London: 1961.

Flusser, D. "A New Sensitivity in Judaism and the Christian Message," *Harvard Theological Review* 61 (1968) 107-127.

Gärtner, B. *The Temple and the Community in Qumran and the New Testament.* Cambridge: 1965.

Guttmann, A. "The End of Jewish Sacrificial Cult." *Hebrew Union College Annual* (Cincinnati) 38 (1967) 134-148.

Harrelson, W. *The Celebration of the Feast of Booths According to Zach. XIV, 16-21,* in *Religions in Antiquity,* ed. J. Neusner. Leiden: 1968.

Kosmala, H. "The 'Bloody Husband.'" *Vetus Testamentum* 12 (1962) 14-28.

Mann, J. *The Bible as Read and Preached in the Old Synagogue.* Vol. 1. New York: 1971.

McKelvey, R. J. *The New Temple: the Church in the New Testament.* Oxford: 1969.

Milik, J. T. *Ten Years of Discovery in the Wilderness of Judaea.* London: 1959.

Montgomery, J. A. "Ascetic Strains in Early Judaism," *Journal of Biblical Literature* 51 (1932) 183-213.

Safrai, S. *Pilgrimage at the Time of the Second Temple.* Tel Aviv: 1965.

Segal, J. B. *The Hebrew Passover from Earliest Times to* A.D. *70.* London: 1963.

Simon, M. *St. Stephen and the Hellenists in the Primitive Church.* London: 1958.

Spiegel, S. *The Last Trial.* New York: 1967.

Suttcliffe, E. F. *The Monks at Qumran as Depicted in the Dead Sea Scrolls.* London: 1960.

Van Goudoever, J. *The Significance of the Counting of the Omer,* in *Studies in the Jewish Background of the New Testament,* ed. O. Michel et al. Assen: 1969.

Vermes, G. *Scripture and Tradition in Judaism.* Leiden: 1961.

Chapter 4

Flusser, D. "A New Sensitivity in Judaism and the Christian Message," *Harvard Theological Review* 61 (1968) 107-127.

Gärtner, B. *The Temple and the Community in Qumran and the New Testament.* Cambridge: 1965.

Vermes, G. *Scripture and Tradition in Judaism.* Leiden: 1961.

Wolfson, H. A. *Philo.* 2 vols. Combridge, Mass.: 1962.

Chapter 6*

* Editions of the major documents of rabbinic literature are indicated in the Appendix.

Friedmann, M., ed. *Seder Eliahu rabbu and Seder Eliahu zuta (Tanna d'be Eliahu).* Vienna: 1902.

Kadushin, M. *Organic Thinking: A Study in Rabbinic Thought.* New York: 1938; *The Rabbinic Mind.* New York: 1952.

Moore, G. F. *Judaism in the First Centuries of the Christian Era: the Age of the Tannaim.* 3 vols. Cambridge: 1950.

Weiss, E. H. *Dor dor we-dorshaw.* 5 vols. New York-Berlin: 1924.

Chapter 7*

* See the literature cited above in the bibliography to Chapter 3.

Buber, S., ed. *Siddur Raschi.* 2 vols. Berlin: 1910-1911.

Davidson, I., Assaf, S., and Joel, B. I., eds. *Siddur R. Saadja Gaon.* Jerusalem: 1941.

Hedegard, O. D. *Seder R. Amram Gaon.* Lund: 1951.

Idelsohn, A. Z. *Jewish Literature and its Development.* New York: 1967.

Oesterley, W. O. E., and Box, G. H. *The Religion and Worship of the Synagogue.* London: 1911.

Petuchowski, J. J., ed. *Contributions to the Scientific Study of Jewish Liturgy.* New York: 1970.

Schechter, A. I. *Studies in Jewish Liturgy.* Philadelphia: 1930.

Werner, E. *The Sacred Bridge.* London-New York: 1959.

Zimmels, H. J. *Ashkenazim and Sephardim.* London: 1958.

Chapter 8

Abelson, J. *The Immanence of God in Rabbinic Literature.* London: 1912; *Jewish Mysticism.* London: 1918.

Husik, I. *A History of Medieval Jewish Philosophy.* Philadelphia: 1916, 1941.

Malter, H. *Sa'adyah Gaon: His Life and Works.* Philadelphia: 1921.

Myer, I. *Qabbalah: the Philosophical Writings of Solomon ibn Gabirol ... and their Connection with the Hebrew Qabbalah and Sepher ha-Zohar....* Philadelphia: 1888.

Neumark, D. *Jehuda Hallevi's Philosophy and its Principles.* Cincinnati: 1908.

Rosenblatt, S., trans. *Saadia Gaon: the Book of Beliefs and Opinions*. London: 1948.

Scholem, G. G. *Major Trends in Jewish Mysticism*. New York: 1964.

Chapter 9

Bensimon, A. *The Zohar in Moslem and Christian Spain*. London: 1932.

Bokser, B. *From the World of the Cabbalah*. London: 1957.

Cordovero, M. *The Palm Tree of Deborah*. Translated by L. Jacobs. London: 1960.

Goinsburg, C. D. *The Essenes, Their History and Doctrine; the Kabbalah, its Doctrine, Development and Literature*. New York: 1956.

Schechter, S. "Safed in the Sixteenth Century," in *Studies in Judaism*, 2nd series. Philadelphia: 1908, pp. 202-306, 317-328.

Scholem, G. *Zohar: the Book of Splendor*. New York: 1949.

Sperling, H. and Simon, M., trans. *The Zohar*. 5 vols. London: 1931-34.

Waite, A. E. *The Holy Kabbalah: a Study of the Secret Tradition in Israel*. London: 1929.

Chapter 10

Bentwitch, N. *The Jews in Our Time*. London: 1960.

Dresner, S. H. *The Zaddik: the Doctrine of the Zaddik according to the Writings of R. Yaakov Yosef of Polnoy*. London-New York: 1960.

Halpern, R. *The Idea of the Jewish State*. Cambridge, Mass.: 1961.

Horodezky, S. A. *Leaders of Hassidism*. London: 1928.

Malter, H. *Shabbethai Zebi b. Mordecai*, art. in *The Jewish Encyclopedia*, vol. 11. New York: 1905, pp. 218-225.

Newman, L. *The Hassidic Anthology*. New York: 1934.

Philipson, D. *The Reform Movement in Judaism*. New York: 1967.

Rabinowicz, H. *A Guide to Hassidism*. New York: 1960.

Rabinowitsch, W. Z. *Lithuanian Hassidism*. London: 1970.

Raisin, J. S. *The Haskalah Movement in Russia*. Philadelphia: 1913.

Sachar, H. M. *The Course of Modern Jewish History*. London: 1958.

Appendix

Primary Sources

Blackman, P. *Mishnayoth.* 7 vols. London-New York: 1951-63.

Braude, W. G., trans. *Pesiqta Rabbati.* New Haven-London: 1968.

Charles, R. H. *The Apocrypha and Pseudepigrapha of the Old Testament in English.* 2 vols. Oxford: 1963.

Danby, H., trans. *The Mishnah.* Oxford: 1933.

Dupont-Sommer, A. *The Essene Writings from Qumran.* New York: 1962.

Epstein, I. *The Talmud Babli.* 18 vols. London: 1961.

Etheridge, J. W. *The Targums of Onkelos and Jonathan ben Uzziel on the Pentateuch.* 2 vols. New York: 1968.

Finkelstein, L. *Sifre on Numbers and Deuteronomy.* New York: 1969.

Freedman, H. and Simon, M., eds. *Midrash Rabba.* 10 vols. London: 1939.

Gaster, T. H. *The Dead Sea Scrolls in English Translation.* London: 1964.

Hadas, M. *The Third and Fourth Books of Maccabees.* New York: 1953.

Harris, J. R. and Mingana, A. *The Odes and Psalms of Solomon.* 2 vols. Manchester: 1916-1920.

James, M. R. *The Biblical Antiquities of Philo.* London: 1917.

Josephus, Flavius. *Complete Works.* Translated by Thackeray, H. St. J. et al. 9 vols. London.

Kisch, C. *Pseudo-Philo's Liber antiquitatum biblicarum.* Notre Dame, Indiana: 1949.

Lauterbach, J. Z. *The Mekhilta of Rabbi Ishma'el on Exodus.* 3 vols. Philadelphia: 1933-1935.

Mandelbaum, B., trans. *Pesiqta of Rab Kahana.* New York: 1962.

Philo Judaeus. *Complete Works.* 10 vols. Colson, F. H., ed. Cambridge: 1929-1962. *Supplements* 1 and 2. Marcus, R., ed. Cambridge: 1953.

Sperber, A. *The Bible in Aramaic.* 4 vols. Leiden: 1959-1968.

Stenning, J. F. *The Targum of Isaiah.* Oxford: 1949.

Vermes, G. *The Dead Sea Scrolls in English.* Baltimore: 1962.

Secondary Sources

Abrahams, I. *Studies in Pharisaism and the Gospels.* 2 vols. New York: 1967.

Black, M., ed. *The Scrolls and Christianity.* London: 1969.

Bowker, J. *The Targums and Rabbinic Literature.* Cambridge: 1969.

Büchler, A. *Types of Jewish-Palestinian Piety from 70* B.C.E. *to 70* C.E. New York: 1968.

Cronbach, A. *Jewish Worship in New Testament Times,* in *Interpreter's Dictionary of the Bible.* Vol. 4. Nashville: 1962, pp. 894-903.

Daube, D. *The New Testament and Rabbinic Judaism.* London: 1956.

Davenport, G. L. *The Eschatology of the Book of Jubilees.* Leiden: 1971.

Davies, W. D. *The Setting of the Sermon on the Mount.* Cambridge: 1964.

Eichrodt, W. *Theology of the Old Testament.* 2 vols. Philadelphia-Westminster, Md.: 1961, 1967.

Eissfeldt, O. *The Old Testament: an Introduction.* New York: 1965.

Herford, H. Travers. *Talmud and Apocrypha.* New York: 1971.

Hughes, H. M. *The Ethics of Jewish Apocryphal Literature.* London: 1909.

Jellicoe, S. *The Septuagint and Modern Study.* Oxford: 1968.

Jongeling, B. *A Classified Bibliography of the Finds in the Desert of Judah.* Leiden: 1971.

Metzger, B. M. *An Introduction to the Apocrypha.* New York: 1957.

Milik, J. T. *Ten Years of Discovery in the Wilderness of Judaea.* London: 1959.

Montefiore, C. G. *Rabbinic Literature and Gospel Teachings.* New York: 1970.

Murphy, R. E. *The Dead Sea Scrolls and the Bible.* Westminster, Md.: 1956.

Newman, J. *Halachic Sources from the Beginning to the Ninth Century.* Leiden: 1969.

Petuchowski, J. J., ed. *Contributions to the Scientific Study of Jewish Liturgy.* New York: 1970.

Ringgren, H. *The Faith of Qumran.* Philadelphia: 1963.

Rowley, H. H. *The Relevance of Apocalyptic.* London: 1963.

Russell, D. S. *The Method and Message of Jewish Apocalyptic.* London: 1964.

Schürer, E. *A History of the Jewish People in the Time of Jesus Christ.* 5 vols. Edinburgh: 1885-1890.

Smith, M. *Tannaitic Parallels in the Gospels.* Philadelphia: 1951.

Strack, H. L. *Introduction to the Talmud and Midrash.* Philadelphia: 1959.

Von Rad, G. *Old Testament Theology.* 2 vols. New York: 1962, 1965.

Wicks, H. J. *The Doctrine of God in the Jewish Apocryphal and Apocalyptic Literature.* New York: 1971.

Wolfson, H. A. *Philo.* 2 vols. Cambridge, Mass.: 1962.

Wright, A. G. *The Literary Genre Midrash.* Staten Island: 1967.